About this book and this teaching...

This publication contains the original account of the principles employed in the creation of our planet by the Builders of the Universe, also called the Seven Elohim. These principles of precipitation are part of the eternal Law of Life. They apply to the creation of a planet and to present-day conditions, such as increasing our financial supply or gaining in spiritual development. Man, as Co-Creator with God, may utilize these rules advantageously in his daily affairs.

The teachings contained in the books distributed by the Ascended Master Teaching Foundation are based on the instructions of Divine Beings, also called Ascended Masters. Jesus, Mary, Moses and Confucius are among them. A new phase of their teachings commenced in 1930, when the Ascended Master Saint Germain appeared to Mr. Ballard on Mount Shasta. These instructions were supplemented in the 1950's, when G. Innocenti received additional data.

Ascended Master Teaching covers a wide range of subjects; there are approximately 15,000 pages of original dictations. The instructions are a practical guide in reaching the goal of all life, namely the gaining of mastery over energy and vibration, and the achievement of the ascension. Solutions are offered to mitigate today's planetary crisis, which will affect everyone. This teaching is for those individuals who are searching for the highest aspect of truth.

We are grateful, indeed, to be able to bring this book, which has been out of print since 1957, to the attention of the reader.

The

Seven Mighty Elohim

Speak

ON:

The Seven Steps to Precipitation

Presented by

THOMAS PRINTZ

Ascended Master Teaching Foundation
Mount Shasta, California

DEDICATION

This book is lovingly dedicated to the Seven Mighty Elohim of Creation, Whose co-operative endeavors created the planet Earth, as well as all the planets of this Solar System. Our book is also dedicated to those spiritually-minded men and women who desire to learn the Science of Precipitation and Etherealization from the Elohim Themselves; to those who will use the knowledge so attained to build and re-create upon this Earth the glorious Kingdom of Heaven which was here in the beginning and which shall now be the Permanent Golden Age for this planet and all Its evolutions.

The Seven Elohim are mighty Beings of Love and Light Who responded to the invitation of the Sun of this System and offered to help to manifest the Divine Idea for this System, created in the minds and hearts of our Beloved Helios and Vesta —God and Goddess of our physical Sun Itself. Through ages of time, the Elohim have learned how to successfully use the creative powers of thought, feeling, spoken word and action as God intended them to be used from the beginning and, in co-operative endeavor, the Elohim drew forth our entire System in perfect manifestation, of which System the Earth is just one small planet.

i

Upon the Earth today, one of the great requirements of the lifestreams evolving here is to raise
them out of human limitations, which mankind
have drawn upon themselves by the forgetfulness
of their Source, Its Divine Plan of perfection for
them and how to fulfill that Plan. The only way
to permanently raise any lifestream out of limitation of any kind is to teach him how to transmute
his "old" *causes* of distress by the use of the Violet
Fire and then set into action new causes (mostly
invisible) which will create new effects for him
in this physical appearance world, expressing as
opulence, peace, good health, wisdom—on and
on—ad infinitum. No type of subsidy and no
means of security is ever permanent until it flows
forth from the consciousness of the individual
himself; because the gifts from any other members
of the race are the *effects* of the benefactors' consciousness and, thus, only temporarily loaned to
the beneficiary.

So, to enrich the consciousness of the individual
until he becomes Master of his own energy within
himself and learns to create *causes* which will manifest as these constructive *effects*, the Elohim
graciously have chosen to present to mankind the
Science—the way and means—by which They
achieved the manifestation of our Solar System.

Call to these Great Elohim in all the sincerity
of your hearts! Daily invoke Their light and
understanding to come into your own consciousness! Then practice the Science of Precipitation

and Etherealization as set forth in the following pages of this book, omitting no one of the Seven Steps and prove to yourself that man is the Master of his own fate, as well as the Captain of his own soul.

The student should remember always to study the *motive* for which he desires to learn how to precipitate and etherealize. If he is too close to his own personality or too wound up in self-love, such a student may not be able to clearly discern the true motive for his search for precipitating power. However, before and during his experimentation with the Law as presented here, such an one can and should ask for the removal from his own lifestream of the causes and cores of all selfish and impure motives, known and unknown.

Throughout the ages, many individuals have learned a part of the Science of Precipitation but, through selfish and impure motives, the use of their powers has not been permanent and the soul itself has suffered much by the use of this partially developed talent for selfish gain.

Those who want to use this Power of Precipitation for the enrichment and illumination of the entire human race will be blessed indeed and their supply of money and every good thing will constantly increase as they use the knowledge they have gained. This will give them complete freedom from dependence upon others of their fellowmen for the supply of the good things of life.

Then comes the most subtle part of this whole activity—*how will such increased supply and perfection be used?* Remember Me in that day!

Unto mankind We now humbly offer the words of the Elohim Who created the planet Earth—giving Their knowledge as to how They accomplished this great manifestation of perfection; also presenting a way and means by which mankind can become spiritual partners with Them to manifest greater glory on the Earth for themselves and all the evolutions using the Earth as their "schoolroom" at this time!

Lovingly, hopefully, sincerely—

EL MORYA

INTRODUCTION

In January 1986, several students of Ascended Master Teaching received the prompting that there was an urgent need to reach out and present this teaching to additional students. It was decided to simultaneously publish six books, this one included. These books were published many years ago, but unfortunately, were not circulated on as wide a basis as possible. Now is the propitious time to circulate them on a large scale, as the Masters had urged from the beginning. Two books were last printed in 1957, one book (until two years ago) was made available only to members, only two of them were translated, none was available in bookstores.

The material for *The Seven Mighty Elohim Speak* was given by the Seven Elohim through the messenger of the "Bridge to Freedom", Geraldine Innocenti, prior to 1957. Our love and gratitude pour forth to the Seven Elohim, the Seven Archangels and to the Seven Chohans, who, for long periods of time have radiated a particular God-Virtue (Quality) to the Earth.

The reader may achieve the greatest benefit from this radiation by reading dictations of these Great Beings or by wearing the color (a scarf or a tie will do) of the day (see chart). By giving loving attention to these Beings and Their outpourings, the student becomes a magnetizing and radiating center, blessing the entire human race.

The chart has been adjusted to take into account certain changes in the offices of Earth's hierarchy, which took place in 1956. Sanat Kumara was released from his voluntary exile and returned to Venus. Lord Gautama assumed Sanat Kumara's position as Lord of the World, Lord Maitreya became the Buddha, Jesus and Kuthumi filled Lord Maitreya's position as World Teacher and Lanto and Nada filled the vacancies, as Chohans.

God-Virtues Radiated by the Elohim, Archangels and Chohans

Ray	Elohim	Chohan	Archangel	Quality	Day	Color
First	Hercules	El Morya	Michael	Protection, God-Ideas Power and Initiative	Sunday	Blue
Second	Cassiopea	Lanto	Jophiel	Illumination, Wisdom Perception	Monday	Sunshine yellow
Third	Orion	Paul, the Venetian	Chamuel	Love, Tolerance Gratitude	Tuesday	Pink
Fourth	Elohim of Purity ("Claire")	Serapis Bey	Gabriel	Purity, Resurrection, Artistic Development	Wednesday	White Crystal
Fifth	Vista ("Cyclopea")	Hilarion	Raphael	Consecration, Healing, Scientific Development Concentration, Truth	Thursday	Green
Sixth	Elohim of Peace ("Tranquility")	Nada	Uriel	Devotional Worship Minisration, Peace	Friday	Gold and Ruby
Seventh	Arcturus	St. Germain	Zadkiel	Ordered Service, Culture, Refinement, Diplomacy, Invocation	Saturday	Violet

PREFACE

There exist many different strata of consciousness into which mankind "tunes" the mind. For instance, kindergarten children are all more or less interested in the activities presented to them by their teachers, parents, guardians and associates. In like manner, patriots tend to "tune in" to the consciousness of all patriotic inclinations—contemporary, as well as those which have achieved certain perfections of government in the past; scholars "tune in" to the consciousness of all teachers, past and present; people with humanitarian interests are brought together by their likeness of endeavor; architects, scientists, ministers, spiritual pioneers,— all are drawn by the magnetism of common interest to the strata where others, thinking and working along similar lines of constructive activity, draw their inspiration and impetus toward accomplishment.

This is equally true with regard to the Higher Realms of Light which are defined in various ways, according to the spiritual, religious, racial and personal development of the individual and collective groups seeking Truth.

Each lifestream's consciousness is like a cup and the vibrations which enter into his consciousness will have an affinity to the vibrations of his own world. Therefore, the finer and more spiritual the consciousness of the "receiver", the more perfect the reception of Truth into that consciousness, where it is either developed and given forth for the blessings of mankind or it remains a dream or vision unfulfilled.

There are certain lifestreams in embodiment upon the planet Earth today who have been prepared over a period of many, many embodiments to receive into their consciousness the higher vibrations, instructions and guidance from Celestial Beings; then such lifestreams present to their fellowman the Truths given to them by Superior Beings for the blessing of all. Some do this through music, through art, through writing, through lecturing and the various media afforded them (by circumstance and co-operation of others so interested in a similar endeavor), thus choosing to be pioneers into the "spiritually unknown".

The individual seeking guidance must use the God-given gift of discrimination to test the instruction! The strata of consciousness which is reached by any spiritual pioneer and his fellow-servers will be determined, primarily, by the purity of such an one's motive; as well as by the capacity to receive into his brain consciousness and translate into words, the Divine Truths actually projected from the Higher Realms through the outer consciousness of the "receiving center". It is as mechanical as the radio or television—

except for the factor of the personality of the "receiver"—which factor, of course, does not exist in the radio or television.

For many ages, during various physical embodiments, such individuals have been able to contact these Divine Beings through the up-reaching of their consciousness . . . and the Truths thus revealed and presented through the various media afore mentioned are the result of such endeavor.

The Seven Elohim Who volunteered to co-operate with the Sun God and Goddess of Our System (Beloved Helios and Vesta) have so used such an individual to direct Their instructions to the mankind of Earth who wish to benefit by the knowledge of how to use the Science of Precipitation and Etherealization which the Elohim used in the creation of this Planetary System. This book is the result of such spiritual research and the consciousness of the reader will truly determine how much or how little of the light of the Elohim he can and will accept at this time. For reasons of eliminating personality, the "receiver" of this instruction has been asked to remain anonymous . . . for it is the gift, rather than the channel through which it flows, that will be of blessing to the people of Earth. As soon as a personality is placed, like a shadow, between the instruction and the Instructors, there is always the tendency on the part of the student to judge the instruction by the habits and nature of the personality. Man does not ask the source from whence water flows; nor from whence the Springtime comes; nor from whence comes the harvest which he gleans. He just enjoys the gift! So let it be now! Accept and use the gift here given—enjoying the fruits thereof!

THOMAS PRINTZ

THE CROWN OF THE ELOHIM

Upon the forehead of every individualized God-intelligence there is a beautiful crown of Light upon the front of which are seven Flames in the colors which represent the Seven Rays of the Elohim.

The First Ray is represented at the left side of the forehead by the Blue Flame of Hercules; then follows the Sunshine-yellow Flame of Cassiopea; then the Pink Flame of Orion.

The center Flame on the front of the Crown is the Crystal Flame of Cosmic Christ Purity, within which is held a focus of the All-Seeing-Eye of God. Around this Flame there ascends a radiance of the Ray to which the individualized life-stream belongs. Next there follows the Green Flame of Vista; the Golden Flame of the Elohim of Peace, ending on the right side of the forehead with the Violet Flame of Arcturus.

As each Elohim, Archangel and Chohan pours forth the radiation of His Ray on the successive days of each week—beginning with the Blue Ray of Hercules on Sunday, each of these Rays on the foreheads of mankind is successively nourished and expanded.

This "Crown of the Elohim" of which we speak is not visible to the average physical sight of un-ascended mankind but It may be clearly seen by any and all who have their true "inner sight" well developed and, of course, It can be and is always seen by the Cosmic Beings, Ascended Masters and the Angelic Host Who minister to mankind. This "Crown" is a natural God-gift of Light to every God-intelligence incarnated and is the anchorage of the Seven Rays of the Elohim in every brow. When well developed, this "Crown" is a certain protection to the brain structure and mental body, as well as a focus for the "inner sight" of the individual through the raising into God-activity again of the pineal gland in the center of the brain. The anchorage of these Seven Rays into the forehead of each individual gives the Elohim, Archangels and Chohans an "Open Door" through which They may give assistance to mankind.

When the sincere student of Truth becomes conscious of this "Crown" (having accepted Its presence upon his forehead by receiving the Masters' instruction to that effect) he also accepts each day the radiation of the Virtues of the Great Beings concerned therewith. Consciously "tuning in" to that Virtue through his attention upon Them, much more concentrated blessings are rhythmically received by such a chela.

These Seven Rays on the forehead act like a spiritual "antennae" magnetizing the gifts of the Seven Rays into the individual worlds of those who will consciously accept them. Then, according to Divine Law, this lifestream sends forth the blessing received, amplified by his own conscious direction.

Anyone who wishes to daily use the following Chant to the Seven Mighty Elohim will find a sense of tremendous balance coming into his life and experience right here in this physical appearance world. To get the best results from Its use one should practice It at least once every day at about the same time.

The musical notes for the chanting of the Name "E-lo-him" are the following: F below Middle C, followed by the next full tone G—then B flat. The Word—"I AM"—should be spoken in one's ordinary tone of voice—then follow immediately by singing (with a musical instrument if possible) the tone of F (below Middle C), then G and then B flat. This activity should be repeated seven times, focusing the attention each time upon the Rays and Names of the Elohim in order, beginning with the Blue Ray of Hercules on the left. The Chant goes:

"I AM"! E-lo-him! E-lo-him! E-lo-him! E-lo-him! E-lo-him! E-lo-him E-lo-him! Seven times seven— "I AM" E—lo—him!!

The words "Seven times seven—"I AM" should also be spoken in one's own voice tone—and the final E-lo-him taken on the three musical tones— this last time very slowly!

The blessings of the Holy Spirit are upon you always—as you T R Y!

Lovingly

Maha Chohan

xiv

IMPORTANT!

May we alert our Gentle Readers to the fact that the inversion of the Sixth and Seventh Chapters of this book IS NOT AN ERROR! The reason for this unusual arrangement is clearly explained in several of the addresses of the Beloved Elohim.

OUR LOVE TO ALL THE ELOHIM

Our song of love 's to all the Elohim—
  Blest Hercules, with Flame of Blue;
To Cassiopea, Flame of Wisdom;
  And dear Orion, of God's love so true;
Beloved Elohim of Purity;
  And Mighty Vista, Heaven's Son;
To Elohim of Peace eternal;
  And dear Arcturus—LOVE TO EVERY ONE!

Thou Master-builders of Creation—
  From Whom came Earth, Air, Sea and Skies;
To Thee we sing our adoration—
  Our Friends of love, so patient, strong and wise!
We thank Thee for Thy ever-presence,
  (Thy Ray is anchored in each brow);
Let all Earth's evolutions bless Thee
  With gratitude and praise—ACCEPT THEM NOW!

Our "I AM" Presence—Heavenly Father—
  Help us like Elohim to be;
Reveal Thy Plan Divine and help us
  To now fulfill It most obediently!
By Violet Fire remove obstructions
  And quickly now make all things right;
Enfold in Elohim protection
  All God's creations—RAISE THEM INTO LIGHT!

Our gracious Alpha and Omega,
  Our Helios and Vesta dear!
Flood now Thy oceans of perfection
  To our great Elohim for service here;
And to their Complements of beauty—
  Magnificent beyond compare—
All blessings of God's love enfold Them!
  Make Earth victorious—THIS OUR EARNEST PRAYER!

MELODY: *Original*

CONTENTS

CONTENTS

xviii

These Blessings Are for You ⟝

GENTLE READER:

Now, since it is the great and impersonal desire of all Ascended Beings of Light and Love Who have set Themselves eternally free from every human limitation by the use of these same Laws which They now so graciously offer us for use so that we may enjoy a like accomplishment, will you please—every Gentle Reader of this book—just consciously, joyously, lovingly and gratefully *accept* for yourself, individually and personally, every blessing recorded upon the following pages which were originally given to those who were privileged to hear these words for the first time. *Please do this* and have the tremendous assistance which those blessings will bring into your daily experiences, right here in this physical appearance world. *Accept them as though they were meant for you alone* and then USE THEM for the blessing and freedom of your fellowman. Thus you will be of such tremendous assistance in *being* and *expanding* "The Light of God That Never Fails", individually for yourself and collectively for all; setting our dear Earth and all Her evolutions more quickly free. Thus, too, will you be able to say with Beloved Jesus: "I AM the Light of the world"!

Hercules

Beloved Elohim of First Ray

(WILL TO DO; DECISION)

Divine Complement— (*Feminine Counterpart*)

Amazon

HERCULES BELOVED

Hail! Hail! dear Elohim Hercules!
Let all adore Thee on bended knees!
Great God of Power and Love and Light—
  Thy glorious Blue Flame, in God's "I AM" Name,
Brings Victory's might.

Blessed Hercules—
  We love Thee—Great and Holy One—we love Thee dearly;
Elohim so bright—
  We love Thy Light which teaches us the Law so clearly.
Come to Earth today—
  Release us all from that which never God intended!
Take Thy dominion—
  Transmute and raise and purify and free forever all that
    lives on Earth today!

Teacher of men and of Angels too—
  We welcome Thee and Thy Flame of Blue!
Master beloved of our Morya dear—
  We're grateful indeed—Thy Presence we need—
We welcome Thee here!

Friend of ages past—
  Whose blessed Ray is anchored now in every forehead;
Come! and claim Thine Own—
  Compel Thy wisdom and instruction to be heeded!
Loose Love's power now—
  Into and through each one within the New Endeavor;
Compel perfection
  And God-supply and God-control and everything that brings
    God's Plan fulfilled for all!

To Thee—Great Hercules, Lord of Light—
  We give ourselves in Love's great delight!
Use us as Rays from Thy blessed heart—
  In Pink, Blue and Gold, Thy glory unfold—
Make shadows depart!

Amplify our calls
And bring us instantaneous proof of God-in-action!
From Thee Victory flows—
Releasing everything that brings God-satisfaction!
Angels living here
Rejoice to feel and know Thy freeing, loving Presence;
And Elementals—
Their happiness and joy are boundless at the sound of Thy
dear voice resounding clear!

Glory of Love from our blazing Sun—
Bless our dear Hercules, Heaven's Son!
Bless His Beloved with glory too—
O, Great Central Sun, bless Heaven's Great One
For service so true.

Blest Creator Dear—
Let all within and on our Earth call Heaven's blessings!
Precious Lord of Life—
Thy power of Love in tenderness is all-caressing.
All life everywhere
We call to sing with us in gratitude eternal!
Bless Thee forever
For countless ages of Thy gifts of courage, strength and
power Divine to free all men!

MELODY: *Adapted from "Soldiers' Chorus" from the opera
"Faust."*

1

*I*N the Name of God, I bring you the FIRE of Hercules!

I AM the Elohim Who embodies the WILL TO DO! I AM the Elohim of DECISION—and God spare me the vacillating man! Everything that has ever been accomplished on the plane of Earth or in the plane of Heaven has been accomplished by men and women of Decision; by Angels, Elementals and Devas of Decision; by Beings Who have voluntarily chosen to combine the energies of Their lives with the WILL TO DO! *Without that WILL TO DO, there is no permanence of accomplishment!*

Preceding all action; preceding all manifestation, *there must be the WILL TO DO within the consciousness.* In this Universal Scheme, it is My privilege and honor to embody the fire (enthusiasm) and the WILL TO DO that which God intends. It is My joy, My privilege and My honor

4

this morning to bring to you the pressure of My love and Flame of My heart; to expand upon your foreheads My Presence, Consciousness and WILL TO DO what God intends!

Are you content with what you are; what you manifest today? Are you content with half a loaf when you could have a full one? Are you content to live in limitations and bodies of decay? *It is what you WILL that you manifest!*

FIRE, O God! the Flame of Decision upon the foreheads of these who are yet the best of the fruits and harvest of My Ray and Kingdom on the Earth. FIRE them with the WILL TO BE what Thy great heart would have them be! FIRE that Flame upon their foreheads until they WILL to be the opulent, precipitating Presence; until they WILL to be the dignified embodied youth of God; until they WILL to set aside disease, decay and death and *know* LIFE; until they WILL to embody uninterrupted harmony in the energies of their being.

No longer shall the Heart of Hercules represented by certain chelas embodied on Earth, WILL to abide in shadows! Shame! FIRE them with the remembrance of their God-estate, O God! FIRE them with the WILL to become manifest expressions of God-control to all the sons and daughters of men—Masters—*not victims*—of circumstance!

FIRE them to see with the sight of God! FIRE them to hear the Celestial Voice of their Presence! FIRE them to move upon the Paths of Light!

FIRE them to manifest the Healing Presence by the release of the radiation of comfort and peace which flows from "the hems of their garments"! FIRE them to reject the lethargy and discordant creations of the mass consciousness of the race!

O, beloved students of Light! *Upon your forehead blazes the Flame of Hercules!* Remember It each morning, acknowledge It before you proceed into the activities of the outer world and WILL TO BECOME THAT WHICH GOD INTENDS!

I am honored to be the first of the Elohim to bring to you today some knowledge of Our activities; to set into motion a rhythm in this series of addresses by which you may have for yourselves and give in printed form to the world (as you have so graciously done with the activities of the Archangels) the seven-fold service of the Mighty Elohim of Creation,—which is an individualized process of precipitation. This you can embody in your own mental consciousness to externalize that which you require.

Precipitation—Its Power Your Birthright

Beloved ones, We have come to a point where you who are the builders of the New Age must enter into the science of creation. The slip-shod happenstance; the hopeful, faithful consciousness taking the bitter with the better, *is not enough!* Such consciousness must be succeeded by a scientific process of creation through your individual

mental and feeling worlds by which you become
and remain Master! Then you channel for Us into
the world of form, those ideas and patterns which
will create the nucleus of the Permanent Golden
Age which your great Master, Friend and Patron,
Saint Germain so desires to make manifest.
Through whom shall this Age come but yourselves?
At this time, Saint Germain has no one else embodied here through whom He can work but
yourselves—those who love Him and have served
Him through the years. *You are the open door!*
Have you thought that through? This means that
your mind is a channel through which must be
lowered the ideas that fill the Realm in which
He abides and then through your minds, vitalized
by your feelings, they must be precipitated into
manifest expression for the blessing of life. Therefore, your minds may be trained in the use of the
powers which are the gifts of the Elohim. Follow
Me closely, now, please!

The Seven Steps to Precipitation

In all creation, where the Mighty Elohim embody Their Seven-fold Flames and Rays, there are
seven "steps" to precipitation—seven consecutive
processes. Each One of Us (the Elohim) embodies
the masterful use of one of those "steps":

First: Preceding all manifestation comes the desire—then the DECISION and WILL TO DO!
Preceding all activities in the outer world of form,

you, too, first desire and then make a decision to use your life to endeavor to externalize some pattern or plan. I represent that activity to the Elohim.

Second: Following Me, the Mighty Cassiopea gives the gift of PERCEPTION (ILLUMINATION)—the capacity to cognize the idea; to grasp it; to meditate upon it; and to draw forth the ways and means which will enable you to bring it most quickly and satisfactorily into form.

Third: After you have perceived, we come to the service of the Mighty Orion—DIVINE LOVE —the power of cohesion which draws the unformed into form. This is the power which draws primal life into the pattern or idea held in mind and sustains it there as long as desired.

Fourth: Then comes the activity of the Mighty Elohim of PURITY—the Beloved Claire. His action is to hold steady the clarified picture, not distorting it by any opinion or desire of the outer self; being a pure, clean pane of glass (as it were) through which that perfect idea is drawn down as a matrix; then filled in with light-substance and perfected.

Fifth: Next comes the activity of the Beloved Vista ("Cyclopea" as some of you have been calling Him), holding the CONCENTRATION (CONSECRATION) of the energies until the design is completed. His service is that which enables the mind to hold to the pattern and not fly off at a tangent to some other plan or scheme; the channelling of the energies; the holding of the pattern until it is wholly completed.

Seventh: Then, for the purpose of precipitation, the activities of the Sixth and Seventh Rays are inverted and the Mighty Arcturus comes in now with the USE OF THE VIOLET FIRE, RHYTHM OF INVOCATION and PRECISION; the planing; the filing; the smoothing—perfecting the symmetry of the form.

Sixth: When it is all but completed, the activity of the Elohim of PEACE (Our Beloved Brother "Tranquility") takes the form, increasing it in beauty, harmony and service; sealing it within His Flame of Cosmic Christ PEACE. This enables the creation to be permanently sustained. Everything which is created in Heaven's Realm immediately begins to expand into greater and greater perfection and service. This is just the opposite of your activities on Earth for here, as soon as something is born or created, it begins to disintegrate and decay unless, by conscious knowledge and use of the Law, some self-conscious intelligence definitely commands its sustaining by conscious decree.

If you were to take up this pattern of precipitation and apply it to your every-day life—this pattern which We use in the creation of Suns, Stars and Systems of Worlds, you would see and experience the *scientific rhythm and precision* of creation according to the Divine Plan. Follow Our procedure through for the precipitation into

form of some constructive idea or thing which you
desire to bring into manifestation; first, of course,
asking your Holy Christ Self within to give you
the picture of the perfect pattern or design of that
which you wish to bring forth. You see, the primal
idea is first accepted in the DECISION (WILL
TO DO) of the heart; it is then PERCEIVED and
studied in all its beauty; it is then drawn forth by
LOVE; held PURE by the one-pointed consciousness of PURITY; then, through the power of
CONCENTRATION it is nourished and fed;
through the RHYTHM and symmetry of decree
and application it is perfected; and through Divine
PEACE it is sustained and expanded as a gift which
can live for Eternity.

Importance and Power of the WILL

Beloved ones, if you were to *concentrate* upon
the Law as We give It, you could come from a consciousness of limitation into one of complete freedom very quickly. It all depends upon how much
you WILL TO BE; YOU WILL TO DO and
YOU WILL TO BECOME!

As Lord Buddha sat in contemplation, searching
for the fullness of Truth, it was His WILL which
drove His consciousness up through every Sphere
until He reached what He considered to be the
"Ultimate". It would not let Him abide long
in the pleasures of any Sphere of beauty which
was less than the full perfection of the Heart
of the Eternal. When He stood in the Presence

of the Angels; when He heard the songs of the Celestial Choirs; it was His WILL which enabled Him to forego the happiness and freedom of staying in those Realms. His WILL drove His consciousness through into the Heart of Truth. When He finally did stand consciously in the Heart of Truth and *realized Himself there* in that God-free estate, it was His WILL again which brought His consciousness back to Earth in order that He might give to mankind the Truths embodied in His experience.

It was the WILL in the hearts of Joshua and His followers which brought down the Walls of Jericho as they marched around them. It was the WILL in the heart of Jesus Christ which enabled Him to walk that road to Calvary; which burst the tomb asunder and which enabled Him to ascend into the fullness of His perfection (His Ascension) in the presence of some five hundred.

In the case of Saint Germain, at the time of His embodiment as Columbus—one fearless and determined man among many fear-ridden and doubting sailors—it was HIS WILL which carried His groaning ship, the Santa Maria, across the ocean. It was the WILL of the early patriots which brought forth America as a Land of Freedom.

That which a man WILLS—*he shall have;* for the WILL is the magentic power of the Godhead in the heart which does invoke and bring to man that which he desires.

One day, on a small island in the North Sea

(Ireland), one man (today known as St. Patrick)
stood praying earnestly for His people. He stood
there in the Sun, in the rain and in the windy gale
and even the coming of the Mighty Cosmic Being
Victory could not make Him desist. Mighty Victory said to Him: "Patrick, descend again and do
not press God further". Patrick, unmoved answered Him: "I WILL to remain here until I have
the word of Almighty God that my people shall
not know spiritual death!"

Again came the Great Victory and said: "Patrick,
go down from this hill in peace". Patrick again
answered Him: "I WILL to remain until my
prayer is answered". Finally, He did receive that
for which he had prayed.

It was the WILL of Moses on Mt. Sinai which
brought to Him the Ten Commandments. It is
YOUR WILL which has brought you to what you
are today. You have used but such a small part
of It! Ah, children, God's WILL for you is the fullness of all good; all opulence; all beauty; all freedom! Give Me the man or woman *who will
not accept a partial payment from life!* He who
says in the calm dignity and mastery of his own
heart: "I WILL to be God-free"; he who holds
his chin up, straightens his spine and proceeds
along life's way refusing death; refusing dissolution; refusing poverty, limitations and chains;—
such an one is Hercules embodied!

How long has man said *with lips alone:* "Thy
Kingdom come; Thy will be done on Earth as it

is in Heaven"? *One man meant it*—and, *for Him it was!*

I FIRE you today with the realization that what you WILL to be, YOU WILL BE! What you WILL to manifest, *must come,* for it is Law!

Beginning of Earth's Creation

When the great Helios and Vesta were endowed with the power to create a Universal Scheme, They first called forth the Silent Watcher and, into Her great Cosmic Heart, placed the light pattern of the planets of the System They desired to create. Then They summoned the Elohim and Builders of Form. I, representing Them, came and said: "We WILL to do Your will. We WILL to externalize Your pattern and plan. We WILL to bring forth from the bosom of the Silent Watcher that which God and Your gracious Selves desire".

Then the Beloved Cassiopea, casting the golden beam of His wisdom into that pattern, helped Us to PERCEIVE the glory of each planet as God intended; the mountains, the rivers, the trees, the atmosphere.

Next the great Orion brought the Flame of DIVINE LOVE (COHESION) by which We drew, each in turn, the light pattern from the bosom of the Silent Watcher. Then We drew out of Universal substance the necessary ingredients to make the globe according to the Divine Design.

All the time, the great Flame of PURITY held

inviolate that Design so that not one mountain; not one tree; not even one blade of grass should be conceived out of *Our* minds (the Elohim) but all was made manifest according to the purity and clarity of the design of the God-parents of this System.

After this came the radiation of the Beloved Vista, holding that CONCENTRATION of energy; channelling it; calling the powers of the Builders of Form, the Angel Devas and the mighty Directors of the Forces of the Elements to serve until it was completed.

O, the great power then of Arcturus, planing and perfecting in RHYTHM of Invocation and Music until each tiny part shone and made the whole appear like a many-faceted diamond. When the creation was completed, it was set into motion by Our Brother "Tranquility" (Elohim of PEACE) through the Three-fold Flame within His heart. The planet began its revolution as the radiation of His PEACE flowed forth.

We, the Elohim, as the Universal Builders, have the Universal light substance as Our canvas; the Causal Body of the Great Central Sun as our paint; the Cherubim, Seraphim, Angel Devas and Builders of Form as Our brushes; the creation of Planets, Stars and Systems as Our work. The Music of the Spheres is the sound of the energies of Creation as they do their perfect work and all is done in such joy; in such harmony and perfection! That is how you, too, beloved ones, must one day create.

Seven Fold Plan of Creation is Universal

From the tiniest Elemental—the tiniest conscious being who desires to evolve, up to the greatest Cosmic Elohim Who works with Galaxies of worlds, the seven-fold pattern of creation exists. This Elemental, tiny as he may be, must WILL first what he chooses to do,—whether it be to design the smallest buttercup, the feathers of a bird or a willowy blade of grass. Then he must PRE-CEIVE the pattern which is held by the Deva Who is the Teacher in his schoolroom; he must have the power of LOVE within him to draw Universal light into his tiny pattern; he must have a clarity and PURITY of consciousness which does not choose to make a design different from that which can be of use in conformity with others. For instance, in the grouping of apple blossoms, if one decided suddenly to make a pear or cherry blossom in the grouping, he would be of no value to that particular pattern. Therefore, holding the PURITY of the design is so important, as well as the selfless serving, even in the tiny Elemental. Then come the CONCENTRATION,—holding to one pattern until it is completed. Next comes the PRECISION—the perfect symmetry of form so that the petals are even and the perfume pours out from it just as it does from the others representing the same blossom; finally it is all sealed within the PEACE which gives that radiation to life.

In the Angelic Kingdom, exactly the same rule holds sway; the WILL to embody some of the nature of the feeling of God; the PERCEPTION of the Great Being Who represents and radiates that feeling; the LOVE which draws and holds that particular form together; the PURITY which does not change the quality, even for another good one; the CONCENTRATION which holds the feeling long enough so that it may be carried to an ailing child, a distressed parent, or wherever the need may be; the PRECISION in symmetry and RHYTHM of the release of that quality so that it can be a permanent blessing and so that it does not suddenly burst forth all at once but is gradually released for the benefit of those for whom it is intended; then comes the expansion of that radiation and its sealing in PEACE. The same procedure of creation takes place in the human kingdom, do you see?

It follows such an orderly pattern and plan. Those of Us Who have lived to create form for a Planetary System have been drawn into the atmosphere of Earth at this time because the theatre of Earth, as you know, is presently the Host to all Beings Who are desirous of bringing Her back to Her Divine Design before the Cosmic Hour when this Universe moves forward into greater light.

Group "Forcefields"—Greatest Hope for
Establishing New Golden Age

We are more grateful than words can tell that you have invited Us and given to Us your "forcefield", that through it We may give to many thousands of the people of Earth an understanding of Our specific service in the Universe. My Brother Elohim will follow Me in addressing you, each One in turn, enlightening you as to His particular service in the creative scheme. Then, if you wish, you may have this instruction put into printed form for distribution to the people of Earth as the gift of the Elohim. Through your devotion, you have already drawn forth the Presence, radiation and instruction of the Archangels, which is now also available in printed form.

In your innocence, you do not yet understand fully the importance of a "forcefield" to the Ascended Master Octave. It is a "pull" upon Our energies, which "pull" cannot be denied! That "forcefield" is proof to the Cosmic Law that there are embodied individuals who are interested in Our service to life; making an open door for Us through which We may give Our assistance to unascended mankind. It is also a radiating center so that when We do come closer into the atmosphere of Earth, Our gifts, radiation and power of accomplishment are not confined to the few who hear Our words but they become planetary in their blessings to the people.

Since the Atlantean days, these "forcefields" have been few and far between. On rare occasions, when great Beings like the Buddha, Beloved Jesus and some of your Saints took embodiment on Earth (before the victory of their Ascension had taken place), *Their auras were such "forcefields"* for the release of radiation from the Ascended Masters' Octave, as They allowed Themselves to become selfless "conductors". Thus Their personal auras rendered a very definite service to mankind. However, the conscious, scientific creation of a permanent "forcefield" through the energies released by groups of individuals in decree, song, visualization and contemplation, is one of the greatest hopes for the establishment of the new Golden Age upon the Earth; with the minimum of cataclysmic action taking place and with the opportunity for Us to enter into the affairs of men *before,* rather than *after,* world changes occur.

May I say to you whose lives are woven into this Activity here: Do you know that I can trace every one of your lives—your energies charged into this "forcefield" through the years—by your own electronic pattern and the color of your Ray? Ah, sometimes you wonder if your individual presence really means so much in the co-operative group. Sometimes you wonder if you would be missed! If you could see, as I do, each one of those "ribbons" of light representing each one of your lifestreams,—each time you are absent that particular "ribbon" does not have opportunity to increase in momentum in the same manner as the others and the "forcefield" as a whole is therefore denied the blessing of your life.

As I settled into the comfortable radiation of your "forcefield" this morning, I confess I was amazed at the power and positive control of harmoniously qualified energy which has been drawn thus into the atmosphere of Earth. Even though I had heard about it from Others Who had previously visited you, it was an amazement to My consciousness.

Remembering Hercules as you move forward now, please do not accept such great limitation in your individual selves, *when you know it only requires the exercise of the WILL within you* to draw forth ALL—ALL THAT YOU REQUIRE!

I WILL TO BE GOD-FREE!

In the Name and by the power of Hercules, I WILL TO BE GOD-MASTER!

In the Name and by the power of Hercules, I WILL TO BE A GOD INCARNATE!

Say it with all your hearts! Mean it! If Buddha and Jesus did it; if Mother Mary and Kwan Yin (Goddess of Mercy) did it; if Moses and Saint Patrick did it; cannot you? Ah, yes, My children! You are the pillars of Hercules! You are Myself in action! God bless you!

Cassiopea

Beloved Elohim of Second Ray

(PERCEPTION; WISDOM; ILLUMINATION)

Divine Complement— *(Feminine counterpart)*

Minerva

GLORIOUS CASSIOPEA

Cassiopea, Elohim,
  Lord of Wisdom's Flame!
Flood the Earth with Love Divine,
  Into Your Light all claim!
Past perfection, glory, too,
  In Your heart are sealed;
Future greatness planned for all,
  Is by Your Light revealed.

Love 's the Master over all,
  Power of Wisdom's Flame;
Love will answer every call
  Made in the "I AM" Name!
Love is purifying fire,
  Bringing freedom here;
In God's Love we welcome You,
  Cassiopea, dear!

Love's great Pattern—"*Good*" for all—
  Is by You perceived;
By obedience to that Plan
  Is His Design achieved.
In the forehead of each one
  Does Your Ray abide;
Make it now a dazzling Sun—
  Stay close to each one's side.

Cassiopea, Elohim,
    Let all men know Truth;
By Your Victory let all win
    Heavenly gifts of youth.
Let all shadows disappear—
    Gone forevermore;
By Your Light to all now be
    Heaven's Great Open Door!

Glory of Creation's hour,
    Holy Elohim—
Bring "I AM" creative power—
    Life's miracles begin!
Saturating all with Love,
    Harmony and Peace—
Let all live in Wisdom's Way;
    Mastery to all release!

God resplendent, Holy One,
    You we bow before;
Gratitude Supreme we bring,
    Loving You evermore!
From the Central Sun on High,
    Call we blessings here;
Flooding You with gifts of Love,
    Cassiopea dear!

MELODY: "Moonbeams Shining" from "The Red Mill" by
Victor Herbert (Key of B Flat).

22

2

I AM Cassiopea—Elohim of PERCEPTION and WISDOM; Elohim of the concentrated power of attention, without which the mind could conceive and know nothing, here or hereafter!

The power of your attention, beloved ones, is the open door to your mind and your entire consciousness. On the beam of your graciously directed attention I came earthward this morning, bringing into the compass of your sweet planet the energies, the powers and the light; as well as the wisdom, the understanding, the comprehension and the PERCEPTION of the Elohim which you may choose to accept and use. Later, it may be written into the substance of Earth and published in printed form,—through your consecrated energies. In this way, all mankind may learn of the activity of the Second Ray from the aspect of the Builders of Form, the Creators of the Universe and Those who work on the Second Ray with Me. Our Ray brings illumined understand-

23

ing of God's Divine Plan and Design; His Pattern
to the people of Earth who open the door through
their attention to that Pattern and Design.

Vital Importance and Magnetic Power of Attention

Beloved ones, in the outer consciousness, *you
do not realize yet how powerful a force is your
attention!* At this time, the attention of the Cosmic Beings, the Ascended Masters, the Angelic
Host and the Devas has been directed toward the
planet Earth by the God-parents of the System because of the great need and requirement of the
hour. This need is to awaken those interested to
an understanding of Earth's place in Our Solar
System and of the requirements of the current
hour for Her redemption and eternal victory in
the light. That Cosmic attention (which is a
beam of directed, concentrated light, looking not
unlike the serachlight beam which you see playing over your great air-fields),—that concentrated
beam of energy from the intelligences of the perfected Beings is now playing upon the planet
Earth and has aroused the sleeping spiritual centers within yourselves, as well as within the more
advanced and developed of the sons and daughters
of men. This Cosmic beam has awakened your consciousness and spiritual self, the Immortal Flame
within your heart, from the soul-sleep of the
ages and has caused to stir within you a desire to
return to your Celestial Home.

The planet Earth is presently in a state of Cosmic incubation and the beams of intelligent energy (which you call Cosmic Light) ,—are really light substance consciously directed to the Earth by the attention of Cosmic Beings upon Her.

One of these beams is the golden Flame of Divine ILLUMINATION from the hearts of certain of the Hierarchy which has been directed to this Earth for some time. As Illumination's Ray has continued to play upon the Earth and as the attention of the advanced members of the race has begun to reach out again toward God, the return current of the attention of the mankind of Earth to Heaven made the circuit complete.

We have loved and watched over you for so long! *Our attention has been upon you for a much longer period of time than your attention has been upon Us!* Through Our attention to you has flowed Our love and desire to help stimulate you to a point where you would begin the search for spiritual Truth; where you would begin to realize that the play-things of the senses no longer gratified. So you have discovered that the ordinary course of living and dying, as well as satisfying the personal nature, was not enough! Then your attention began to turn again toward your Source and even the most feeble beam of that attention, connecting with your Source, brought in response a greater outpouring of Divine love and light from above.

Now we come to the great Cosmic Hour where

your conscious attention is drawn to various members of the Hierarchy, according to a perfectly designed Plan, presented by Lord Maitreya, the Great World Teacher,* in co-operation with Beloved Saint Germain, Beloved El Morya and Beloved Kuthumi.

As your attention is turned toward the Hierarchy; as the names and activities of various Beings are brought to your mind's eye, so does your attention become a magnet which draws from the Octaves of Perfection certain Beings; certain activities of the Sacred Fire and certain God Intelligences Who use your life, through the beam of your attention, to enter into the lower atmosphere of Earth for the blessing of mankind! *Without your attention upon Us, there is little We could do for you.* Your conscious, directed attention through your songs, visualizations, contemplations and your mighty decrees made it possible for the Archangels to break the silence of the ages. Now they have also made it possible for Those of Us Who represent the Builders of this Universe to enter into the atmosphere of Earth. So, now I say to you in sincerity and with deep love and devotion—God bless you for your continued attention upon Us through the years,— forming the magnet which has drawn Us into this atmosphere today! God bless you for your atten-

----

* Lord Maitreya has since become the New Buddha; Beloved Jesus and Kuthumi now are serving jointly as New World-teacher.

tion upon the power of God,—which attention draws more and more of that power into the lower atmosphere of Earth, blessing all life!

Creative Service of Second Ray

When speaking to you recently, the Beloved Hercules told you that the first activity of creation is the making of a *personal* DECISION TO DO! No activity takes place on Earth or in Heaven until the intelligence with free-will decides within himself to WILL TO DO and to accomplish.

In the creation of this Solar System, when the Beloved Helios and Vesta (God and Goddess of our physical Sun and God parents of this System) willed to manifest the planets of this System and the evolutions which would some day achieve the victory of their Ascension from those planets; when These Beings so willed within Themselves, the Beloved Hercules summoned Us—the Seven Mighty Elohim. He asked Us if We desired to co-operate in bringing forth the planets of the System and, *as one*, We said: "We will so to do! We *desire* so to do! It is Our voluntary *decision!*"

Following the activity of desiring to do the Will of God; to co-operate and use Our Own voluntary energies in externalizing these glorious planets, My service came to the foreground. My activity is that of perceiving what the God-parents had designed and wanted to have made manifest. The purpose of the Second Ray is the PERCEP-

TION and active, illumined contemplation of the God Plan and Design. After you will to serve God; after you have made the decision and the surrender to the Will of God in the Secret Place of your own heart, next you must receive the Divine Idea, the directions as to how to manifest It and that portion of the God Plan which your own Christ Self would have you formulate and externalize. In exactly the same manner, We, the Elohim, Whose service to life, mind you, *is constantly creating* Planets, Stars, Suns, mighty focuses of light,—We had to become still enough to put aside the constant activity of creation in Our Own minds and feelings *to be able to know what Helios and Vesta desired.*

Therefore, the first activity of the mental body, after making the decision TO DO, is to become still; to stop the creative processes in honor of and in homage to the God Beings concerned or to one's own God Self and look upon the pattern and plan of one's Superior. In your case, this would be your Holy Christ Self and the Ascended Master Who is working with you. In Our case, it was the God-parents of the System.

Think for a moment of the power of creation which is vested in Hercules! Every Star in the Milky Way was created through the WILL TO DO, by the consciousness of that Great Being, Hercules,—and you have no count of their number! Yet, in the Presence of Helios and Vesta,— while yet Stars and Planets were evolving out of

His mind and feelings,—His first activity was to stop the motion of His creative centers and look upon the light pattern of the planets held within the bosom of the Silent Watcher, placed there by the God-parents. It was the same with each one of Us,—I holding the golden beam of PERCEPTION for Us all.

Looking upon the Divine Plan of Helios and Vesta, We were enabled then to decide within Ourselves how each one of the Seven of Us might best contribute the wealth, momentums and strength of Our Own particular Ray, to externalize perfectly the pattern of the God-parents. *We did not choose to change it according to Our Own Design,* but gave freely of Our life in illumined, humble obedience, to make of this Solar System the most glorious and perfect manifestation ever known!

Divine Purpose and Use of Mental Body

Now, beloved hearts, your mental body was created for just such a purpose. Your mental body was created to be a magnetic field, through the power of your attention, to draw into itself Divine ideas from your Holy Christ Self, or from some Ascended Master Who has taken particular interest in you and uses you as a part of Himself in the world of form. There are many individuals incarnate today who have voluntarily chosen to become partners here with an Ascended Master;

a Brother working in one of the Etheric Cities;
or someone of great light who is working at Inner
Levels between embodiments. Although the latter are not incarnated on Earth at this time, they
can and *will* lower into the mental body of the
incarnate lifestream so willing, certain ideas which
have been perfected at Inner Levels. Through the
concentrated beam of his attention, the Brother
from the Inner Realm will hold that pattern within the mind of the receiving one until his own
feelings, physical energies and good common sense,
coupled with consecutive rhythm of decree and
invocation, can externalize it.

These Masters, Brothers and the unascended
working at Inner Levels to whom We have referred
above, are dependent upon the reception into the
mental body of the embodied one, of Their beam of
light through his attention upon Them, or the idea
which They are trying to manifest through him.
Your Holy Christ Self is likewise dependent upon
the reception into your mental body of the directions which should naturally arise from the Golden
Plume of the Three-fold Flame within your heart
into your brain consciousness. Your Holy Christ
Self should be the complete directing Presence of
your every outer expression. The *natural, normal
activity* of the human self is to *completely rest* in
the serenity and control of the Flame within the
heart; the Three-fold Flame of Love (pink),
Wisdom (gold) and Power (blue). That Golden

Flame of WISDOM carries within Itself the directions of the Holy Christ Self to the outer consciousness and should be constantly in control of the mental vehicle; constantly precipitating into it the Divine Ideas which the Great Ones choose to channel through you. When those ideas come, it is the responsibility of the mental body to hold them clear enough and long enough for the feelings to breathe into them life; breathe into them love; breathe into them enthusiasm and, through that pressure of light, externalize them into the world of form as manifest substance.

Need for Purifying Mental Body

Now, wherefore do you fall short of this? I will tell you, beloved ones! Your mental bodies, which are supposed to be these clear, magnetic fields of conscious energy, are so filled with the accumulated concepts of millions of years of living, that the Divine Ideas have no place to take root. You have seen a plowed field in the Springtime with the Earth newly turned, waiting for the seed to be planted which will bring forth a harvest in its time. You have seen a field which has not been so cultivated but, instead, is filled with weeds waist-high. You know well that should seed be sown in such a field, there would be very little within that field to nourish and bring a harvest to fruition. This is the condition of the mental bodies of the race in general today. Instead of being ready to receive and fecundate the Divine Ideas from the Holy Christ Self (like the plowed-open field) receptive to and desiring to do that Will alone, mankind's mental bodies, through their attempts to satisfy the appetites of the senses, have been sown with tares, weeds and every conceivable human concept. Therefore, the Holy Christ Self (through the Flame in the heart), the great Masters of Wisdom and those who seek to reach mankind through their mental bodies, find not—even among the conscious chelas—that open, receptive, pure, consecrated and concentrated upheld Chalice of mind into which to plant the Divine Idea.

Your mental body receives through your attention and through all the activities of the senses. Everything your attention connects with—good or otherwise—draws back into the mental body a picture and form into your mind. If it be discord, whether you see it, hear it, feel it or whether you draw it in through any of the activities of the sense consciousness,—that discord enters the mental body and adds to the accumulation which is there! The mental bodies of mankind are like an old warehouse in which has been stored the furniture and accumulations of the ages. They are full of cobwebs and discordant human concepts; as well as much that is petrified and some which is in the process of disintegration!

In the course of an average life, mankind accepts "hit or miss" from the atmosphere; from the current religion of the day; from the educational system of the time; from the parents to whom he is born; from the race to which he belongs; from the history which he reads,—certain pictures which add to this conglomerate mass in the mental body. Through the qualification by the consciousness and experiences of each lifetime, the energies of each successive embodiment keep pushing backward into the past accumulations of the mental body, which consist of all that has been previously recorded. Through this conglomerate mass We endeavor to drive perhaps *just one* grain of Truth! Into this, from time to time, We endeavor to plant, perhaps *just one* seed and *hope* it will be nourished and grow.

Beloved hearts of light, when you first received your mental bodies from the Heart of Creation, they were so pure and beautiful! They were like the crystal ball which the fortune-tellers use (unfortunately, may We say) to magnetize the pattern of the future for you. However, in their original purity, those crystal balls of light signified the condition of the mental body which received from the Holy Christ Self the clear, concise, beautiful ideas of perfection. Then the outer self, perceiving that idea, realized that it came from God and that it was given into the keeping of its mental body; then to be nourished by the feelings, developed in beauty and externalized in form. Now We must bring you again to that state! That requires the purification of your mental vehicles from ages and ages of imperfect accumulation! The great Golden Flame from My heart is given to you freely to render this service for yourselves. Even as I am speaking to you today, I am passing My Flame through the brain consciousness of every member of this race incarnate and all those who are yet awating opportunity to embody!

Please LET GO! LET GO! LET GO! of your *human* concepts of the ages. Ah, beloved hearts, Truth is a discomforting Presence! So many of mankind, seeking knowledge, wisdom, education, —seek only confirmation of their own concepts. In all honesty, have you ever noticed yourselves, —when reading a book or paper,—how you love to come upon that which confirms something which you hold dear within your own conscious-mind? You know how disconcerting it is when a new idea is driven at you and disturbs the peace of your concepts! Beloved ones, it is not the service of Perfected Beings to confirm any human concept. It is Our service to bring you pure, uncolored, Cosmic Truths which, if applied, will give you your Eternal Freedom! The men and women of open mind are those who, receiving into the mental body the Key to Freedom, apply It and walk upon the Pathway of Light into their Eternal Victory!

Stilling the Mental Body

Well, We take you just where you stand! First and most necessary for those who are to become the "Way-showers" for mankind, is the stilling of the mental body. When We enter a room as I did here this morning and We look upon the eagerness of the chelas to understand, the first thing that is noticeable is the motion of the inner bodies. Mankind in the West do not know how to become "still"; "still" in an alert, awakened anticipation which is not lethargy, sluggishness nor a negative consciousness. Before We begin to assist you, Our endeavor is to pass the Flame and Ray from Our Own consciousness through your minds and feelings. Thus We, at least to a certain extent, are able to still the agitations in your thoughts and feelings to a point where We can pierce through and anchor into your minds perhaps just one idea which you may take home, nourish it by contemplation and bring it to fruition. Have you noticed, as We come again and again, how little you retain of what We say? How much of what We offer you is put into actual application? Yet, you are far above the average consciousness of mankind today. *You are those through whom We hope to reach the masses.*

The first requisite, then, to manifest a Divine Idea is the stilling of the mental body and a desire to perceive the Will of God. The next requisite is purification of your mental body so that all the shadows and discordant concepts; all of the human logic and reason do not intrude upon the purity of the Divine Pattern as It comes into the mental body from God. This purity protects the Divine Idea so that It is not dissolved or literally "devoured" by the many human concepts which have been living there from the past. Then, as you are able to perceive that design in Its purity, the next requisite is the concentration of your energies upon It, so that It may be externalized.

The mental body is two-fold. It is the receptive consciousness into which the Pattern comes; then, it is perceived, accepted and when it has been grounded in the mind, the great creative power of the mental body begins to act in a controlled, channelled and rhythmic manner. It creates around the seed idea the form thereof, cutting out of Universal Light the pattern which is necessary to enable that form to become a manifest expression. Then the mental body summons the feelings and asks the light thereof to flood through that thought-form rhythmically until that form is filled and lowered into etheric substance. From the etheric substance, it is lowered into precipitate manifest form. The rhythm and uniformity of the nourishment of your pattern and design will determine the speed of its manifestation; will determine the quality of your thought externalized; will determine how long it will live in this world of form and will also determine the blessings which such a precipitation will be to the rest of this race.

Beloved ones, will you please begin to follow through this Science of Precipitation? Manifest each day some conscious externalized idea you have received from the Heart of the Father! You must begin this conscious training!

When Beloved Saint Germain brought to you some time ago the activity of the Elemental as the power of creating form; the activity of the Angels as the power of vitalizing form with feeling; the activity of humanity as the power of magnetizing thought and feeling (thus acting as the bridge to externalize it into the world of manifest expression)—He did so with the HOPE that by giving you the knowledge of the exact SCIENCE of creation, you would then have confidence in your own capacity to do these things yourselves. Then, in that confidence, faith and conviction that it is not just happenstance but that it is mathematically accurate and scientifically applicable for all mankind, *you become the Law incarnate!* You are the teachers of the New Day! Believe Me, the teachers of the New Day *will not be accepted on words alone.* They will be accepted on works! *You* are the chosen of the Brothers and Sisters of the Golden Robe Who, in illumined obedience, are to carry this Law to mankind!

How can you convey the Truth of the Law to others *if you do not know how to prove It?* However, prove it you can! You have a Holy Christ

Self and you accept that in the abstract. This Holy Christ Self has access to all of the Kingdom of Heaven; to all of the Seven Spheres. This Holy Christ Self is endeavoring to externalize through you the perfection of those Seven Spheres, according to your particular part in the Divine Plan.

The Seven Steps to Precipitation

When We were first called by Helios and Vesta and asked if We were willing to create this planet Earth, We said:

First: "We WILL to help You!" Next, We had the humility to ask what They wanted Us to do.

Second: Then, We were given that PERCEP-TION, when We looked upon Their Divine Design.

Third: We also had the Divine LOVE to magnetize electronic light substance to form the planet.

Fourth: We had the PURITY and humility not to desire to change Their Divine Design.

Fifth: We had the CONCENTRATION of energy to stay with it (and do you know just how many millions of years it takes to create a habitable planet?).

Seventh: We also kept the RHYTHM of invocation and many a day We left Our Own particular Cosmic work to join with the Others of the Elohim, pouring love and light into this planet which was taking form at that moment. Never was one of Us missing at that rhythmic hour, lest the Flame of Cassiopea or, perhaps, the Flame of Orion, should be in smaller proportion to that of the Others. If that had happened, the perfect harmony and balance of the Seven Elohim which came in rhythm century after century, would have been broken.

Sixth: Then it was required of Us to release to and through Our creation the PEACE and harmony which would sustain this planet until Its evolutions began upon It; as well as after the creation of mankind who were invited here to enjoy It.

Your Holy Christ Self now awaits your recognition and acceptance of It—and *not in the abstract!* That Holy Christ Self is a *very real* Being! *It* awaits opportunity to show you your Divine Pattern· which can be revealed to you through your mental consciousness, when it is held like a Grail to that Holy Christ Self. This must be done in humility, sincerity and in a realization that, certainly, the Being Who made you and has sustained you for millions of years,—giving you even yet the breath of life—that Being should at least have some "say" in your affairs!

Joyous Enthusiasm Essential for Success

When It is afforded opportunity so to do, the Holy Christ Self will press into the mental body certain portions of the Divine Plan through flashes of inspiration during periods of exaltation. The outer self should accept that,—not in a sense of strain; not in a sense of human will; but in a sense of great love for that Being Who has guarded and guided you, giving you life through the ages. When you get that feeling of complete consecration; that feeling of surrender within yourself; that desire to be about the "Father's business" first and foremost; and when you determine consciously to let go of everything else, *that instant your outer self will know it!* Then, when the Divine Pattern (Divine Idea) comes to you, you should let your feelings *enjoy* fulfilling It! How many men and women make that surrender; see the pattern which is to be their destiny; and yet, the feeling body shrinks from co-operation with that Holy Christ Self. Such an outer self then withdraws from the surrender; the Divine Idea is still-born and no manifestation occurs.

There is no unascended being who has not passed through that experience at least once during the span of his lifestream. Even in Gethsemane's Garden, the greatest of men asked that the "Cup" be taken from him! However, I warn you that, *unless the feelings rush joyously and enthusiastically* into the Plan to externalize It, your precipitation will be either lifeless or of very little lasting value to yourselves and to the world. When your feelings confirm your desire to do the Will of God and then you do that Will *joyously,*—in decree work, visualization and the

"Father's business" becomes a vital activity which fills the feelings with happiness and opportunity to serve,—then your creation becomes something which lives long after your own course is finished and you have returned "Home".

If Our energies had been poured reluctantly into this planet Earth, She would not have been such a beautiful shining Star as She was in the beginning; Amaryllis would not have found Her such a lovely workroom into which to weave Her energies, bringing the perfection of Spring; and the Angels Themselves might not have been magnetized. We created in love; *in great love and joy* and in anticipation of mankind's presence and happiness here!

Beloved friends, take now opportunity! Take now these great promptings and prepare yourselves to channel into the world of form some good and lasting blessing to life. Do this in Our Name and when you get that confidence which comes with your first conscious precipitation of substance into tangible, manifest form direct from the Universal, do not rest on your oars! Go right ahead into greater and greater experimentation with the power of your mental body to create form; your feelings to give it life; your etheric and physical bodies to channel it into the world of manifest expression. DO THIS and BE the precipitating Presence, remembering the Golden Flame of Cassiopea which is yours to use *and freely!*

Within your heart is the Golden Flame of ILLUMINATION which will reveal truth to you. Now, in answer to My call, this Flame arises into your brain structure and outer consciousness, clearing away forever the human concepts of the ages; clearing away forever half-truths and expanding the Golden Flame of the Seven-fold Activity of the Elohim, which is anchored within your forehead. Thus, if you will consciously accept it, each one of you is being made a Grail through which some Perfected Being may channel and direct His blessings for the race.

For Saint Germain, let us become the Precipitating Legions! For Saint Germain, let us become the Peace-commanding Legions! For Saint Germain, let us become the Healing Legions, as you here, in great power, already have become the Protecting Legions of this Earth!

The Science of Creation is in your hands and hearts. The Science of Creation is now planted in your thoughts! The Science of Creation must be externalized in your worlds, *if you love Us as you say you do!* Accept it, please! Use it and BE, for all mankind, the Brothers and Sisters of the Golden Robe, in full command of the power of thought, feeling, spoken word and action,—the Elohim incarnate! I thank you!

Orion

Beloved Elohim of Third Ray

(DIVINE LOVE; COHESION; ADORATION AND GRATITUDE TO LIFE)

Divine Complement— *(Feminine counterpart)*

Angelica

GLORIOUS ORION

Glorious Orion dear, Elohim Immortal!
  Flame of Love's great "I AM"—Key to Heaven's portal!
Oceans of Your Pink Flame releasing,
  Holding Earth in Love's balance true—
Enter into our grateful hearts—
  Elohim—we welcome You—all the GLORY of Love!

Love is the Source of all—reason for our being!
  Love answers every call—from all discord freeing;
Love is patient and kind and selfless;
  Love will never *compel* Its Own;
Knowing all It shall ever need—
  Flows from the Father's Throne—this the WISDOM of Love!

Elohim of Love's Pink Flame—used in Earth's creation;
  Call we on Mercy's Flame for Her devastation!
Calling all Light's redeeming power
  Into action for Earth today—
All the glory She had before
  Now takes dominion here—by the POWER of Love!

Third of the Elohim, dear Orion, we love You!
  For You, all Heaven's gifts from the Realms above You!
On and on into Life's Perfection—
  Your dear Loved One and You arise;
Into beauty no words can tell—
  You are, Orion dear—ALL THE VICTORY OF LOVE!

  Melody: "You Are My Song of Love" from Operetta
"Blossomtime", Key of F.

44

3

Oct. 3, 1954

I AM Orion, Elohim of LOVE—that Divine LOVE which has caused to come into being every Sun and Galaxy in the Universe; every Star and every Planet; every form—from the Great Solar Galaxy to the tiniest Elemental and atom belonging to this planet.

Divine LOVE is a *positive* and *not* a negative quality. I come into the atmosphere of Earth this morning on the wings of Divine LOVE, bringing with Me the concentrated Flame of that LOVE. This Flame has been the magnetic cohesive power which drew into being the Earth upon which your feet stand, the very physical bodies in which you presently function and every other manifestation which appears here. Every form which you enjoy is a part of My Being, held together by the Flame of My LOVE; for, if Divine LOVE (which is COHESION) were to cease to be, all in the Universe would return to the

45

unformed and become again part of primal life.

This morning, I bring into the atmosphere of Earth the fullness of that Pink Flame and Ray, individually for you! I bring It as a melting, dissolving spiritual alchemy to remove those resentments and pressures of energy within your feeling worlds, deeply imbedded within your memories. These pressures are caused by the records of many unhappy experiences of the past which have formed wounds and scars within your etheric (memory) bodies. These wounds and scars burst open upon the slightest provocation, spewing forth again the poison of past enmities, past feuds and past misunderstandings.

Man knows not what he carries around with him, buried deeply within that Realm which Science calls the "subconscious" mind; that Realm in which there are atrophied the memories of every experience in every embodiment from the first day the lifestream "fell from Grace" up to the present moment. Sometimes, Those from the God-free Realms Who guard and govern the destinies of World Movements almost shudder when They look upon the ever-weakening scar-tissue which the glorious Builders of Form seek to weave over those hurts and distresses in the etheric body. However, in order to fulfill Itself, the Divine Plan brings together again and again certain lifestreams, each one of whom carries these memories of past enmities between them; the Divine Plan presenting over and over again

new opportunities to "make things right".
Sometimes the very proximity of these individuals to each other (even in Divine service)
will cause provocations to arise which are similar
to those which made the original wounds. Then
these wounds are likely to burst open once more,
tearing asunder the etheric body. This releases
again into action those feelings of rebellion and
buried hates from the past which originally de-
stroyed the comradeship and affinity of these
lifestreams for each other and weakens those ties
which *should* "bind their hearts in wondrous
LOVE".

Beloved ones, will you now *consciously* give
me your *attention*, please? If you know of any
lifestream with whom, in this Earth life, you are
not in complete accord, consciously draw the
image of that person before your mind's eye *now*
and let Me give you the pressure of *My feeling*
of *unconditional* loving forgiveness toward that
one. *If you will accept this,* it will cut you free
from the recoil of the energies of those past mistakes which made the enmity in the beginning.
Experiences of physical embodiment, good or bad,
weave ties that, if they are not worked out here on
Earth, will have to be balanced in another Realm
through your inner vehicles (etheric, mental,
emotional).

This hour, I *blaze* and *blaze* and *blaze* into,
through and around you the most concentrated
action of pure, Divine LOVE, increasing Its in-

tensity and pressure until it will be impossible for you to even retain the memory of injustice or to allow again the stirring of so-called "righteous indignation". *Accept this now and be free!* This is the gift of LOVE which I bring into the heart and world of each one of you who will accept it.

Creation by the Elohim

I am One of Those Whose great joy it is to paint upon the Cosmic canvas, responding in LOVE to Intelligences Who desire to bring into being whole Universes. Our first activity is the making of the DECISION wherein We WILL to comply with the design created by some God-being. Then, We look upon that pattern held within the bosom of the Great Being known as The Silent Watcher and, in order to begin such creation, first We (the Seven Elohim) join together Our energies in LOVE and consecrate them unto the completion of the God-design. We LOVE to use Our life to unfold some portion of the Divine Plan in some Galaxy or System. The great God-parents Themselves (Helios and Vesta in this case), designed a Universe with Their Own hearts and consciousnesses; a series of potential planets, each to provide habitation for the evolutions which were to come forth thereon. These God-parents created that entire design in LOVE. Why did They do this? You have been told that God divided the Rays in order to have something to LOVE. He gave intelligent consciousness to you so that you might share the joy of creation.

When Helios and Vesta had completed that design, it was LOVE in the heart of the great Silent Watcher that answered Their call and brought Her before Them. Then the Silent Watcher accepted into Her bosom Their Divine Design for this particular Universe. She held it within Herself exactly as She received It from Them; until such time as the Elohim (responding also to the call of LOVE), gathered around Her, looking upon the Divine Plan of this creation which She held. For this gigantic task, the Beloved Helios and Vesta summoned to Their assistance the Seven Mighty Elohim.

First, the mighty fiat of Hercules went forth to those of Us Who work as One Body. Said He: "A new System is to be born; a new set of God-parents has chosen to create a series of planets. I am called upon to give the decision as to whether or not the Seven Elohim will choose to cooperate with the manifesting of this Plan. Do you, My Beloved Associates, choose to be a part of this creation?" In answer, each One of Us rushed forth in LOVE—*grateful for opportunity to serve.* Each of Us said: "I WILL!" As Spokesman for Us all, Hercules then preceded Us to the Thrones of Helios and Vesta and, announcing Our decision said: "Beloved God-parents, WE WILL to create Your Universe for You. *What now is Your design?"*

It was LOVE which enabled Us to have the courtesy to accept the design of Those Beings, rather than to project Our Own. Then, in Their great wisdom and light, Helios and Vesta asked the great Elohim Cassiopea to pass His Golden Flame through the body of the Silent Watcher and reveal the magnificent Divine Pattern for this Solar System. We all stood looking upon It with LOVE, interest and admiration; seeing the size of each planet and the number of lifestreams which were to come upon it. In LOVE, We looked upon the hope of the God-parents of this System.

Then, in the activity of My Ray (Divine LOVE), began Our service of creation. LOVE, the Universal Magnet which all life must obey, drew primal life from its quiescent state at My command and, that primal life obediently took form according to the Pattern which We perceived in the bosom of the Silent Watcher. Thus We proceeded in the creation of each planet.

Loving Cooperation in Rhythm

First—there was Hercules' WILL TO DO; then there was Cassiopea's PERCEPTION; then came My LOVE—the focal point—the Immortal Flame within the heart of Our creation. Then came the activity of the Elohim of PURITY, holding true

to the original Divine Design so that, even un-
consciously, there might not be imposed upon this
Pattern some change of form, coming from some
other Galaxy which We were completing at other
hours of the same day. This beloved Elohim held
to the purity and symmetry of the Divine Design
in courtesy to the great Beings Who chose to
bring It forth. Not One of Us would *presume*
to enter upon the creation of the planets of the
System if, in illumined obedience, We were not
willing to follow the Design of Those Who drew
It forth.

Then came the CONCENTRATION of energy
by the Mighty Vista (Cyclopea), so that all the
Elementals, Angels and Builders of Form could
coalesce Their energies and talents around one
planet at a time, when that one was being drawn
forth into form.

This CONCENTRATION of the Mighty
Cyclopea was so important—staying with the
Divine Plan for the Creation of each planet, so
that when the Manu of the First Root Race was
ready and His people were ready to take embodiment, We had not dissipated Our energies in creating something which was more pleasing to Ourselves. Besides, in following the Divine Plan given
to Us, it enabled Us to have planets ready on time.

Then, as the radiation and power of the Mighty
Cyclopea increased, We drew the activity of Arcturus—the RHYTHM of the outpouring of each
of Us. This is one of the most important factors

in creation for rhythm provides nourishment for the form. In your physical bodies, the rhythm of your heartbeat and that of your breath determines the efficiency of the physical form you wear. In your own precipitation, the rhythm which you establish will determine the symmetry, beauty, accuracy, efficiency and general perfection of your manifest design.

For instance We, the Elohim, offered to give a certain amount of Our time each "day" to the creation of this one planet and We all arrived *on time, rhythmically,* no matter where We had been or what We had been doing,—mind you, other Galaxies, other Solar Systems were being created at the same time! Perhaps We had better explain that We do not use "days" in the same sense as you do here; We use the words "days" and "hours" (which scholars question), because We must have some measure of expression which you will understand in order to be able to convey to your minds a rhythm of application.

Our Seven Flames fed Our "infant" planet, breathing into It the Cosmic application of creation. The mighty Devas Who govern the building of form also came in rhythm and gave Their service; the Angelic Host came and gave Their service rhythmically too. The Directors of the Elemental Kingdom and the Elementals themselves also worked in rhythm with Arcturus, the great and mighty Elohim of the Seventh Ray.

Here, again, there is the inversion of the action

of the Sixth and Seventh Rays in the Elohimic activities, so far as the building of planets is concerned. Here the Seventh Ray (representing rhythm) precedes the Sixth (representing peace). The reason for this is that the rhythm of building is a part of the service of the Seventh Ray in order to permit the coalescence of Universal light into form. The Sixth Ray (ministration and radiation of PEACE) is the solidifying of the perfect design. This now takes seventh place so that when the Earth was completed, as It first began Its Own revolutions upon Its axis, the Music of the Spheres began to pour forth from that planet.

Therefore, *lastly* came the radiation of the Elohim of PEACE ("Tranquility") which held the form of the Earth from disintegration because, *where harmony, peace and tranquility abide, that which you have drawn forth cannot either be taken away from you or disintegrate.* Just as you shellac certain things to preserve them against rust and decay, so does the activity of the Elohim of Peace enfold and seal all creations in the entire Planetary Scheme brought forth by the Elohim, for the period of existence designed for that creation by the Divine Plan held in the mind of the Universal First Cause.

Again came the importance of rhythm as the Beloved Amaryllis (Goddess of Spring) brought Springtime to Our Earth successively for nine hundred years. Only then was Our planet ready for habitation.

In this same manner We proceeded with the creation of the other planets of this System. These are the SEVEN STEPS TO PRECIPITATION (creation) used by the Elohim and Builders of Form on a Cosmic scale. You and every individual who desires to become master of the creation of form, *must also learn to use these same seven steps.*

The Seven Steps to Precipitation

First: You must WILL TO DO! You must make a DECISION in your heart, mind and spirit; a decision based upon prayerful thought and application so that *you are sure it is the right decision* and that your feelings concerning it are enthusiastic about bringing it forth.

Second: After you WILL TO DO, take the time to call into action the Flame of Mighty Cassiopea to give you Its PERCEPTION (Illumination) — the perfectly clear picture of what you want to do and the directions as to how best to bring it forth; to qualify the abstract idea so that your form is something of benefit to life.

Third: LOVE your manifestation into form. The more sincere feeling of LOVE you can put into it, the more beautiful will be your form and the more quickly will it manifest. This is true whether it is something you wish to create for your personal use or whether you are altruistic enough to so create for the benefit of a World Movement. The more LOVE you put into your service, the greater will be your manifestation; the higher will be its quality and the more plentiful its blessings to the world of form.

Fourth: Then be sure to hold firmly to the original Divine Design. In as much humility and selflessness as possible, hold to the PURITY of the Pattern (Divine. Idea) which you have received from God and *do not attempt to constantly change it with every passing whim.*

Fifth: Next comes the power of CONCEN-TRATION; following through with one thing at a time; staying with it until it is wholly completed. It is better to do *one thing well* than to do a hundred things imperfectly. Your phrase "Jack of all trades and master of none" refers to this wavering consciousness. *Do not allow fear and doubt or ridicule of the outer world to make you feel that it cannot be done!* When a mental picture is flashed to your mind and you deliberately call it forth *again, you begin to draw forth the reality of that picture.* Your "fundamentals", given to you *for your use* years ago by the Ascended Master Saint Germain, gave you this instruction. For instance, if you want financial freedom *hold to that idea* and see that subsance visible and tangible in your hands and use now. If you want youth in your bodies so that they do not show age and if you want freedom from certain limitations of mind and the flesh body—greater freedom to serve this Cause—*get the definite picture of just what you do want and stay with that one idea until you have brought it forth into outer physical manifestation!* Let there be no "ifs" or "buts" in your consciousness and your Universe concerning it. When that which you have conceived and willed to bring forth hurts no man or any part of life, it will be a blessing to the Universe. If you will LOVE life enough to stay with it; if you will be humble enough to let God do His Will through it; if you will concentrate upon one thing at a time, *you can produce your manifestation!*

(Here, again, comes the inversion of the activities of the Sixth and Seventh Rays).

Seventh: Now your idea which you wish to precipitate into form must be nourished in RHYTHM, with at least as much regularity as you take your meals into your flesh body each day.

Sixth: Last, but not least, when your manifestation finally appears in the purity of form in which you have desired and designed it, *you must hold the* PEACE *and harmony of feeling* which seals your entire creation in Divine protection.

When these seven steps have been completed according to this Divine Pattern, you will see and know that *the creative powers of the Elohim are Universal and can be used by anyone at will!*

Lack of Peace Disintegrates

You know, there was no such thing as disease, decay, disintegration or fermentation before mankind lost their feelings of harmony. Rust, mold,—everything that is unpleasant even in the Nature Kingdom—has appeared because the quality of the Elohim of PEACE ("Tranquility") is not manifest in the form which has been created. Look at the magnificent homes, Temples and cities which have come forth in the past from the minds and energies of man; creations which have crumbled into decay today. Whole continents have sunk from sight beneath the waves of the sea, all because the final activities of Peace and Harmony were not sustained.

In your personal lives, think of the perfection of the body which was given to you at birth. Of course, you cannot consciously remember it but I can tell you it was beautiful—precipitated into the world of form. It would never have known decay or imperfection of any kind if the Flame of Peace had been sealed around it; protecting it from the mass consciousness of disintegration. The activity of *disintegration* is as far from that of *etherealization* as darkness is from light. Etherealization of form (after that form has served its purpose) is a part of the Divine Plan of the Universe. Every Ascended Master or Cosmic Being; every God-intelligence on any Star or System, when wielding the Powers of Precipitation, deliberately wills the length of time through which any form of manifestation shall endure. Then, at His conscious direction, when that form has served its Divine purpose for being, it is harmoniously

and beautifully returned to the unformed without any marks of disintegration, such as odor or
appearances of imperfection. This etherealization
is done beautifully to music and the substance
which has thus served is given a definite blessing
by the Being Who originally drew it forth.

Decaying bodies and moulding form are the
records on the Book of Life of inharmony. Now,
as the Beloved Ascended Master El Morya chooses
to build a New Activity which will be the heart
of a World Movement to make our Earth "Freedom's Star", I tell you truly today that the greatest
wisdom; the strongest will; the most powerful
application will not sustain and expand that New
Activity, unless the feelings of Divine LOVE,
Peace and Tranquility *are held uninterrupted by
those who LOVE these qualities more than they
LOVE having their own way!*

From the time of the "Fall of Man", many,
many magnificent civilizations have come into
being and returned to nothingness because of the
lack of *sustained* Harmony and Peace. Hundreds
and thousands of times all through the ages, you
have drawn forth one physical body after another; only to have them periodically disintegrate
into formlessness after they had served you for
a time—*all because of the lack of sustained Harmony in your feelings and the feelings of those
about you.* (Now, I think perhaps I am projecting Myself into the discourse of the Elohim of

Peace and I should give Him the courtesy of
allowing Him to describe His Own activities in
the Universe. However, since He is such a mild
and harmonious One, Methinks He would not
be as vehement in His plea for sustained Harmony
as I have been here. Perhaps I shock you with
My fiery insistence upon sustained Harmony for
you would not ordinarily expect this from the
Elohim of LOVE.)

Love is Practical Christianity

This morning I come as a messenger of God
to bring to you the activities of Orion (Elohim
of LOVE) and to give you some comprehension
of LOVE as *practical Christianity.*

Precious hearts, it is not the Law that one
should remain in a state of *negative harmlessness*
—a "Pollyanna" consciousness—*that is not LOVE!*
LOVE is a very *positive* quality. To fulfill the
Law, one is required to be *positively good.* Would
it be LOVE for one to stand on a river bank and
watch a man drown? No! LOVE *would plunge
into the stream and bring the man out while
there was yet life in the body.* It was LOVE which
took Lord Buddha from the glorious peace, freedom and opulence of His Kingdom and made
Him walk the paths of Earth, trying to find a way
to relieve His fellowmen from those distressing
appearances of poverty and suffering which

shocked His sensibilities. It was LOVE that kept
Him rising in consciousness through Sphere after
Sphere of God-perfection until He reached the
very heart of Creation Itself. Then He returned
to the limited appearance world and His Own
physical body, in order to bring to His fellowman
the Truths which He had learned in those great
heights.

Let me tell you that after one's consciousness
has been enmeshed in the discord and limiting
appearances of physical embodiment for so many
ages, it takes great LOVE not to succumb to the
beautiful peace of the Inner Spheres after one has
arrived there! Quite naturally, the tendency then
is to just lie down in the first green pasture, saying: "This is it!" It takes a great deal of Divine
LOVE to desire to keep rising in consciousness
from Realm to Realm—pushing ever onward until
one has found the Source of all Truth and then
rest—even if just for a moment—on the bosom
of the Eternal Father. Then—what LOVE it takes
to deliberately determine to come back into this
world of form with its forbidding shadows, after
having successfully made that journey and felt
the beautiful Presence of God, Himself! It was
positive LOVE which brought Buddha's spirit
back to Earth through Sphere after Sphere of
beautiful God-consciousness—back into the hot
burning sands of India, to walk again (apparently
like any other man) just to carry Truth to others.

Love is Action at the Moment When the
Requirement is Greatest

It was LOVE, precious Children of God, which
spurred Moses on to draw the reluctant people
of Israel away from the flesh-pots of Egypt, in
an endeavor to find their "Promised Land". It
was LOVE which made Him walk across those
deserts and, in the extremity of their need, part
the Red Sea which stood between His people and
the protection they desired from Pharaoh's army
which followed them.

It was LOVE which took Moses up the side
of Mt. Sinai when the clouds of discontent, fear
and lethargy of the Israelites had all but put out
the fire of His vision and, sometimes, He knew
not whether He was still a Messenger of God or
whether He had become a victim of fantasy!
It was LOVE which held Him on the pinnacle
of that mountain while God, in His great mercy,
gave Moses the *positive* affirmations of Truth—
The Ten Commandments. Here He received
Them and cut the words thereof out of the very
rock itself. These same Ten Commandments
have remained at least a portion of the Law from
God to man ever since that day. However, through
the shadowed consciousness of mankind, those
Commandments, representing the Divine Law,
have been distorted into the negative form of
"Thou Shalt Not".

It was the LOVE of those who stood with Moses

which upheld His arms at the time when, because
of the very pull of gravity, He could no longer
hold them up Himself in His endeavors to magnetize the power of the Lord to give His people
victory.

In Galilee, it was LOVE that enabled a young
man (with a body of such perfection as has not
been known since on the Earth-plane and filled
with a LOVE of Springtime) to willingly lay that
body upon a cross, submitting to the Crucifixion.
It was LOVE which burst the tomb asunder on
Resurrection morning and LOVE, *again*, which
enabled Our Beloved Jesus to make the visible
Ascension in the presence of some five hundred
people. It was the LOVE FOR GOD which enabled a man who had a greater capacity for affec-
tion and friendship than any of unascended mankind have yet known, that enabled Him to re-
nounce further association with His beloved
Mother and His loved ones, to answer the summons of the Eternal Father—proving that the
conscious Ascension was *possible for all!*

After that Ascension had taken place, it was a
positive LOVE which carried Mary into Bethany
with John, Peter and James and it was LOVE
which enabled Them to establish there the unit
which held the spiritual connection with Beloved
Jesus through all that long period of thirty years
and more before Mary was called "Home".

It is LOVE which brings Lord Michael (the
Archangel) from His Realm of Perfection to serve

in the psychic plane of Earth twenty hours out of every twenty-four, as He has been doing for some years now and it is LOVE which brings the assistance of all the other Ascended Masters and Cosmic Beings into the atmosphere of Earth to answer your calls. LOVE IS POSITIVE CON- CENTRATED ACTION TO ASSIST MAN- KIND AT THE MOMENT OF THE NEED— *according to the receiving capacity of the life- stream which makes the call.*

It is LOVE which sends certain lifestreams to the leper colony, joyously willing to give whatever assistance they can to the afflicted there. It is LOVE which makes the men of research work so persis- tently—often at considerable self-sacrifice—to bring forth those scientific findings which have proven to be of such assistance to the race. It is LOVE, too, which brings the comfort and conven- ience of your inventions into the use of man in his every-day life.

WITHOUT LOVE, NOTHING IS PERMA- NENTLY ACCOMPLISHED; without It the clearest vision remains but a cloudy vapor!

LOVE IS CONSTANCY UNDER THE MOST TRYING OF CIRCUMSTANCES AND AC- TION AT THE MOMENT WHEN IT IS NEEDED MOST.

LOVE was signified by Abraham when He will- ingly laid Isaac upon the Altar of Sacrifice. That which was dearest to Him He offered to the Lord!

LOVE is the pouring forth of the full-gathered

momentum of the good of your own lifestream for the good of all. Let lips be sealed which speak of LOVE if they cannot manifest that LOVE in action—*in service*—not mere words! It was LOVE which brought Me here this morning and LOVE which brought you too—LOVE of God, LOVE of service and LOVE of yourselves; all these entered into it and brought you here.

Recent Blessings to Incoming Children

Now, before We close the address today, let us take up some activities concerning the incoming children and youth, which subjects are so dear to My heart. I am very grateful indeed for the real sincerity with which you have entered into your calls for their protection, purification, illumination and general well-being.

The month of May in each year is the month of consecration of these lifestreams who are to take physical embodiment here on Earth during the ensuing year and it is the time when they all stand before Beloved Mother Mary in Her Temple of the Sacred Heart at Inner Levels. The children who were consecrated in May of this year, of course, are not yet born into the world of form; so you have a little more time to decree upon and develop the "seed ideas" of ways and means to help them—(which "seed ideas" were given you by various of the Great Ones Who have recently addressed you on this subject). By such endeavors, perhaps you can increase the number of perfect bodies and balanced minds which will be allowed by the Great Cosmic Law to be given these incoming children this year for, without your calls, I assure you that some of those bodies would not be so comfortable for them to wear.

Now, at this time, I would like to describe something of what takes place in the physical octave of Earth (while these prospective incoming souls are preparing at Inner Levels for physical embodiment here), especially in, through and around the expectant parents who have a very definite (and sometimes quite detrimental) effect upon the being and world of the soul who is taking embodiment. As unascended lifestreams who are already in embodiment here, (because you are the authority over the substance and energy of the octave in which you abide) you can, if you will, make the calls to the "I Am" Presence, Ascended Masters and Angelic Hosts for the protection, purification, illumination and general assistance to these parents and such calls will assist them tremendously.

First of all, the etheric body is the "memory world" of the individual. It carries the records of every experience in each Earth-life, as well as the experiences at Inner Levels where the soul abides between embodiments. The etheric records of the Earth-life of the individual determine the pattern of the etheric envelope (body) which the soul occupies while it is in the Higher Realms between embodiments. In other words, at the close of an

Earth-life, the Realm to which the soul is drawn for instruction and assistance *between embodiments* is determined by his consciousness at the close of that life—which consciousness is the sum total of his use of life through his own free-will—whether that be constructive or otherwise.

While the soul is in the Higher Realms, the etheric body gradually throws off the appearances of age and disintegration of the Earth-life because, being sustained by a Body Elemental, it mirrors that which it sees and by which it is surrounded. You have been told that all Elemental life is imitative in the extreme. It mirrors anything and everything to which its attention attaches through sight, hearing or any of the senses.* Therefore, when the soul is assigned to a Realm where there is perfect balance and symmetry of form, the etheric body will automatically drop the appearance of age and the distresses of its Earth-life and mirror the more perfect appearance of those with whom they associate in the Temples there; as well as those of the Master Who is their Teacher there.

Each Soul Alloted Its Own "Karma"

However, when it comes time for the soul to come again through the Gates of Birth into the physical octave, it is allotted its "karma" (both good and otherwise) for the next embodiment.

---

* (Note: See final chapter of our book—"Memoirs of Beloved Mother Mary".)

Such "karma" is, of course, the result of all the activities of that soul in its previous Earth-life; as well as in all the other lives it experienced theretofore. The pattern for the new body is determined by this "karma" and the new body's appearance, comfort and effectiveness to the soul is determined by that which the soul has earned in past lives. If many of these etheric records are of a destructive nature, this causes the distortion of the form of the incoming physical vehicle and the Body Elemental copies that "karmic" pattern. You see, the Body Elemental works here with the *etheric* body and, therefore, it would be so helpful to the incoming lifestream if it were to have its etheric body purified—cleansed of all distorted forms and destructive impressions—*before its physical body is builded.*

This morning, We are going to deal with several other phases of this activity which will be beneficial to the granting of the Dispensations of the day and, if your energies are vital enough, I shall ask you to contribute to this service, even though it may be in a small way.

Greatly blessed indeed are the lifestreams of those who are being prepared to be the parents of those incoming souls *who are wanted!* The desire for the child and the parental LOVE which accompanies such feelings, are of tremendous assistance to the lifestream to be born. This LOVE also automatically draws the Deva of the Builders of Form and the Angel (or Angels, in some cases)

Who stand guard around the mother-to-be, particularly during the period of gestation.

However, when you come to the condition where women are bearing children out of wedlock or reluctantly and the qualities of fear, resentment, rebellion and shame are strongly charged into the feelings of the mother, *these destructive feelings have a very detrimental effect upon the mind* (mental body), *brain structure and emotional body* (feeling world) *as well as the flesh body of the incoming soul.* Besides this, the censure of society (which is a great, living, mass "entity" in the atmosphere of Earth) drives its energies against these women and does more to cause unbalance in the minds of incoming children than almost any other one thing—other than their own individual "karma". That entity of which I speak is one of arrogant pride and scorn—terrible in its appearance—and I hope you never have to look upon it! This "entity" forms a pressure of unhappy feeling around the expectant mother and incoming child, against which pressure the Body Elemental must work. A goodly number of those who are to take embodiment this year must face this condition and even now their new bodies are already encased in the substance which is charged with those unfortunate qualities.

I am going to ask you now to sing a song, the energy of which (as it is released by you) We are going to qualify with Violet Fire and dedicate to the melting away of that substance from these incoming souls. At the same time, We shall establish a protective shield of pure etheric substance around both mother and child. In this, We shall be assisted by Beloved Mother Mary (Mother of Jesus), Beloved Kwan Yin (Goddess of Mercy), Beloved Meta (Daughter of Sanat Kumara from Venus) and Beloved Nada (Goddess of Love); all of Whom, last evening, offered to give Their special assistance to these incoming children, if you would so co-operate today by making these calls.

Explanation of "Karmic" Ties

You may ask—and rightly so, too—"Why are incoming souls given (through birth) into the keeping of those who do not want them?" One reason is because of the pressure of the times—a certain number *must be born* within the course of one year, especially now when the planetary evolution is accelerated. You see, "karmic" ties between parents and children often play a very important part in the fulfillment of the Divine Plan—individually and for the planet.

Sometimes a woman will want a child, but when the pressure of the feeling world of the soul she is to bear touches her aura—if her previous association with that soul has been unhappy—a great distaste and dislike for that incoming soul comes into the feelings of such mother-to-be; stirring up memories of past inharmonies with such incoming one. Then the mother-to-be often decides to abort the incoming of this soul because of the tremendous antipathy which karmically binds them together. In such a case, one who had previously prayed sincerely for a child will suddenly not want it.

This is sometimes equally true of fathers-to-be. It is the cause of so many conditions of discordant home-life where fathers resent the children and jealousies ensue. This is because, between the child and the father, there is an old antipathy created by previous discordant associations in other lives—which associations often extend far back into the past. In his outer consciousness, the father-to-be does not realize this and often takes a violent dislike to the child; the mother meanwhile suffering unnecessarily, feeling the lack of the father's love for that infant.

One of Beloved Meta's services to life is to raise up in the world of form those splendid lifestreams who provide places where these unwed mothers are allowed to bring forth their children in privacy, without the censure of society upon them and where these children are given a better start in life. Beloved Mother Mary, Nada and Kwan Yin, as well as many more of Us in Our Octave, also serve with Beloved Meta in this capacity.

Now, I shall appreciate it very much if you will sing one of your songs this morning which will embody the call for the removal of this entity of fear, rebellion, shame and society's censure from the parents—particularly the mothers—who are to bring forth these "unwanted" children. If you will do this, I feel sure that the Great Karmic Board will allow Us to grant these incoming souls much better bodies than they would otherwise have had—even before the activities of the morning are over. (Group sings song to "Beloved Kwan Yin".)

Into the great Coliseum (made of pink marble-like substance, veined with gold) which has been built for that purpose at Inner Levels where souls are awaiting embodiment, this morning We have been able to draw the inner bodies of all those who are to be parents during this coming year. As those great Flames of the Violet Fire of Mercy and Compassion (which have been called forth by you from Kwan Yin, Arcturus, Zadkiel and Saint Germain) pass through their inner bodies, actual sheaths of substance which have been qualified with fear, shame and rebellion, are being transmuted into light. Even as We speak, the Beloved Lord Michael with His Legions, has offered to endeavor to completely dissolve that mass "entity" of scorn!

Sense of Irresponsibility of "Father-to-be" Draws Future Distressing Obligations

Another distressing factor in the environment into which the incoming soul is born is the selfishness and sense of irresponsibility of the fathers— particularly of the "unwanted". That irresponsibility will require such a parent, somewhere, some-day, to take care of that same lifestream again—perhaps the next time under very much more un-happy circumstances and in very great lack; also, the lifestream so cared for may be in very un-pleasant conditions of mind and body.

Individuals who have the care of invalids over a long period of years often wonder what caused this responsibility to fall upon them. Nearly al-ways, it is because, in the past, they were those who walked out on the responsibility of parenthood. Such individuals are bound to meet a "karmic" debt of retribution. So We now ask you to join your energies with Ours in a call to make every man stand by his rightful obligations and become a kindly Saint Joseph—a "Guardian of the Young". (Group sings "Love's Opportunity"). We shall take up your energies so released and qualify them with that which will assist these gentlemen.

As We are watching this activity from Our Realm today, the inner service for which you call is being rendered. These mothers-to-be who are *awake* in their physical bodies at this time are present with Us in their Holy Christ Selves, instead of in their etheric bodies as are the others whose physical bodies are *asleep at this time.* (The etheric body is that in which one goes out in sleep at night). As you sang this latest song, *it is the first time this has happened since the "fall of man":* the incoming lifestream which has been assigned to each set of parents has kneeled before them and

both parents have placed their hands on the head
of that soul, *giving that one the benediction of
opportunity.* The Beloved Venetian and the
Brothers of the Pink Ray are now giving to all
of these concerned an anointing of the Divine feelings of Harmony and Balance and here may I ask
each one of you, individually and silently, to make
the call to the Holy Christ Self of each of these
lifestreams concerned, that the *outer self shall
remember this inner pledge.* You see, when there
is unity of feeling between parents and children,
there can be built a much more perfect vehicle for
the incoming child. (Group sings "O, Mary dear
we love You so . . .")

With such co-operation at Inner Levels, it would
seem that the birth-rate this year will increase even
more than usual, because so many of those who
would otherwise be denied a body (through abor-
tion), doubtless now will get through. Besides
that, We also have the promise of a grant of five
hundred thousand more perfect bodies. These are
to be given to those taking birth this year who
otherwise had better not known birth at all, because of the deformities of mind and body into
which they would have had to have been born.

Now, We are having a very interesting experience in Our Realm this morning. The Master
Paul, the Venetian, has asked the Beloved Maha
Chohan to be present with Us during these cere-
monies and the Maha Chohan asks that your great
petitions continue down into the four-footed king-

dom which has been so much neglected by the prayers and interest of mankind in general and which must now be loved free.

Do you realize just how many unwanted animals are born—for instance, how many "stray" cats there are in one city alone? Beloved Maha Chohan asks that you remember that kingdom from now on. Many, many mothers in the animal kingdom cannot supply enough food to sustain their litters and the Beloved Maha Chohan has applied to the Group Souls Who govern the various departments of that kingdom, asking for the gradual decrease of the size of all litters. This is the beginning of the final removal of animals from the Earth; for the necessity of Elemental life to find the completion of its cycle in an animal form—without an erect back bone and a conscious, thinking mind. God bless you for being a part of this release to them today. I feel that your intensity of LOVE for the animal kingdom will increase as you realize that that form (through the use of the Violet Fire called forth for it by you) will much more speedily evolve into a more constructive expression of life and thereby know great release.

Today, I bring you the full benediction of Helios and Vesta, Sanat Kumara, Lord Maitreya, all of the Elohim and Archangels, all of the Chohans of the Rays and Myself. I also bring you the extreme gratitude of the incoming souls whom you have blessed by your calls; as well as from the Elemental Kingdom. May the Great God Presence of your own lifestream (anchored right within your beating heart) quickly make you know and feel the gratitude of the God-free for such service as you have enabled Us to render, especially here this morning.

Whenever you wish to use and expand the activities of the Third Ray—Divine LOVE—whose qualities are Adoration, Magnetization and Gratitude to Life—I am your Servant! Thank you and Good morning!

Elohim of Purity

("CLAIRE")

Beloved Elohim of Fourth Ray

(PURITY; HOLDING *"Immaculate Concept"*)

Divine Complement— *(Feminine counterpart)*

Astrea

ELOHIM OF PURITY

Hail to Thee, Elohim of Purity!
  God of Creation's pure light;
Coming to Master maturity,
  Earth now aspires to Thy height.
Fourth of the Elohim gracious,
  With power none can excel;
Into Thy heart—heavenly, spacious—
  Come we forever to dwell.

Thou art God's love in Its fullness,
  Anchored within every brow;
In all the worlds of Earth's people
  Take Thy dominion right now!
Purity's the heart of Creation—
  Centralized core of each Ray;
Power and vict'ry's within it,
  Melting all shadows away.

Dazzling, celestial, majestic—
  Perfection most truly Thou art!
God is revealed in Thy Presence,—
  "Blessed the pure in heart"!
Without Thy radiant essence
  Nothing of worth can endure;
"I AM" the call from Earth's people—
  "Make us eternally pure!"

Thy great solicitude ever
  Tenderly answers each call;
Swifter than arrows Thy blessing
  Rushes to heal and free all.
Let now the fire of Thy substance
  Burst forth! Illumine each one!
Let Thy great Flame of Ascension
  Raise all when life's journey's done.

Blessings from Helios and Vesta—
  Elohim of Purity (Claire);
And from the Heart of the Silence—
  Call we love's blessings from there.
Then from the Heart of the System,
  Glorious Great Central Sun,
We call for Thee and Thy Heart-Flame—
  Gratitude—MOST HOLY ONE!

MELODY: Original

4

Nov. 7, 1954

I AM the Elohim of PURITY! Because of your great light, love and interest in "The Light of God That Never Fails" all through the years, I have been invited into Earth's atmosphere again today. I am the Guardian of the Immaculate Concept for this sweet planet Earth, as well as for this entire Universe. I am also the Guardian of the Immaculate Concept of your own individualized Divinity, which is fashioned from White Fire substance and lives in the God-free Realms. This is your Pattern of Perfection originally created by the Godhead and *that Being,* in all Its perfection, *you must one day become!* I am more than this, too. I am the Flame of Cosmic Christ PURITY— the *natural activity* of your own life; not something that must be wooed; not something that must be drawn from without.

79

I am the living, breathing PURITY of the electron which lives in the center of the atom of which your physical bodies are composed. This electron vibrates so rapidly that no discord can enter into or contaminate it. As the substance of My Flame is one with the substance of that electron, then *I am alive in every cell of your body*, moving around the central core of every atom of your flesh, even this moment as I speak to you. Truly can I say with Jesus—"I am with you always!" *I am your life.*

I am the living breathing electronic light of PURITY within your mental bodies, closed in, yes, by the shadows of atomic consciousness; waiting now to be released in order to manifest the perfection of your Divine Conception.

I am the living, breathing Flame of pure light, invoked by each one of you into the great sea of your emotional world; awaiting release to again manifest perfection by the purification of the energies of the atomic consciousness.

I am the pure electronic light within every cell of your etheric garment, upon which you have impressed those records of impurity and I am now expanding My PURITY from within every cell and atom of all your four lower vehicles (emotional, mental, etheric and physical) *expanding, expanding, expanding* My true nature which is the purification of this Earth; all that is in the Earth, on It or in Its atmopshere.

Complete Nature of God in Each Electron

Beloved ones, let us consider electronic light for a moment. If you could stop one electron as it passes through the Universe, or stop it for a moment as it passes from the heart of your Presence into your physical heart, you would see that that electron contained within itself all of the nature of the Godhead; all of Its powers; all of Its majesty *and all of the Divinity which is within the God-parent! The electron itself can never be contaminated,* for My Flame of Cosmic Christ PURITY lives within everyone of them. In the course of a single second, millions and millions and millions of these tiny electrons are literally bombarded from the heart of the Universal First Cause through your God Presence into your physical heart,—then out into your world.

If this be so, from whence comes the shadows, limitations, illnesses, appearances of age and depressions? These discordant appearances are but the "clothing" of those electrons by shadows created from the habit of placing the attention, thoughts and feelings of the outer self upon imperfect appearances in its environment and in the atmopshere of Earth. With your conscious acceptance of My service now, I shall endeavor to remove as much as possible of this shadowed substance around your electrons by the mercy of God and by expanding the power of My Flame of PURITY *which is already within you.*

I speak directly now to the electrons which have come from the Universal First Cause, having answered the call and obeyed the magnetic pull of the Immortal Three-fold Flame within your heart. In and by the power of God Almighty, I now decree that continuous and permanent expansion of that Flame of PURITY in every cell of your bodies. I command this to remove the effluvia (shadows) there and transmute into light every rate of vibration which is an impurity and causes human limitation. I command this done *now* by the most powerful Cosmic action of the Blue Lightning of Cosmic Christ PURITY from My heart which has ever been known to manifest on Earth!

In the Name and by the power of the Great Central Sun of this System which was vested in Me when I was made Guardian of the Immaculate Concept of the sons and daughters of Earth, I decree that the PURITY within the heart of every one of your electrons shall now EXPAND! EXPAND EXPAND! EXPAND EXPAND! EXPAND! EXPAND! EXPAND! EXPAND! until that which appears as limitation can no longer imprison your life in discord and, thus, the shadows cease to be!

Flame Within the Heart—Real "Atomic Accelerator"

Do you know that the greatest "Atomic Accelerator" in the Universe is really that Immortal

Three-fold Flame within your own heart? The acceleration of the speed of the electrons around the central core of the atom within your four lower bodies, is accomplished by the *conscious directing* of that Flame of Life within your own heart? Do you know that when you call for the "Atomic Accelerator" to appear here in multiple numbers for the beneficial use of the people in this physical appearance world (as you have been doing here for years) that the momentums of constructively qualified energy released by this group thus far actually have made its activities to be the first of those "Accelerators",—active on this Earth, actually accelerating the vibratory action of the four lower bodies of the mankind of which you are presently a part? Now, this acceleration released by your calls has been far more powerful than that which would have been released by any *mechanical instrument;* which instrument, however, shall come forth later here for the use of the masses; the pattern having been set by the "Heart of Freedom."

When We enter into the living, breathing "forcefield" which has been drawn and established here all through the years by the release into it of your vibrant, vital energies, what happens? The mighty God-Beings, Angels, Devas and Ascended Masters Who have focused Their energies and vital Rays of light into this room—all this becomes a part of your service to life and adds to the size and radiance of your "forcefield".

The radiation of the pure light substance from These Great Beings, as it comes into the room, accelerates the vibratory action of the electrons of your flesh and inner bodies, just by Their attention focused upon you. As these electrons are quickened in their speed of vibration, there is thrown off the substance of darkness and shadow (created by discordant thoughts, feelings, spoken words and acts of the past) and these shadows are then transmuted into light by the powerful action of the Cosmic Violet Transmuting Flame which fills the room.

O, you who have longed so earnestly to sit within the "Atomic Accelerator" (about which Saint Germain has spoken to you),—remember that these will be provided for the mankind who have not yet learned the mastery of expanding the Flame within their own hearts. However, every time you gather together here; *every time you come within the compass of this "Atomic Accelerator" of Freedom,* there is thrown off from your physical and lower bodies into the Violet Flame so much discordant accumulation that My heart rejoices. This purification also takes place for you, *even when you just direct your attention into this room;* for, "Where your attention is— you are"!

The groups which are willing to abide in the disciplines that We have given; releasing their energies joyously and willingly in decrees, songs and visualizations; thus quickening the vibrations of their four lower bodies; such groups become the acceleration for all in their localities! In the Orthdox world, you have heard much mention of "the quick and the dead". This merely refers to the difference in the rate of vibration of the four lower bodies of mankind (physical, etheric, mental and emotional). The main difference between your unascended bodies and the perfection of Our Own is merely the difference in the rate of vibration of the electrons spinning around their central core in the atom. You see, Our electrons move in an extremely rapid rate of vibration, due to the complete purification of the energies of Our vehicles of expression which We have achieved.

You, too, are gradually achieving this more rapid rate of vibration in your own four lower vehicles (bodies) by the purification you receive from your individual applications of the Law in the use of the Violet Transmutting Flame and other activities of the Sacred Fire; as well as by your participation in the class work.

Purification Necessary for Comprehension

Do you know how much purification is necessary within your mental bodies before you can even *accept Our reality* and Our capacity to speak to you? It would be a source of very great personal gratification if you could see how pure your vehicles had to be before We could even attempt the experiment of coming "through the veil" to speak Our words to you! You see, the vibratory action of the feeling worlds of the masses of the people is so slow (their worlds being filled with all sorts of disbelief and doubt), that even were they to hear Our words, those words would not be accepted by them as Truth; nor would they believe that those words *were actually coming from Us* as Real God Beings. The vibratory action which has been established in your vehicles through all these years of application (individual and in groups) has made possible this spiritual association and partnership today.

Dearly beloved ones, when you are "caught up in the Spirit", so to speak; when you are gathered together here as you are this morning; the vibration of your bodies is raised, each one, to its present ultimate point of comprehension. Then there is anchored into your worlds as much of the substance, energy and vital fire of Our Beings as We know you can individually absorb. What happens next? After the meeting is over and your attention is again upon the things of this world, *you go back into the accustomed vibratory action of your own aura by giving it your attention again* and thus connecting with the effluvia of the individuals with whom you live, with whom you work and the appearances of less than perfection by which you may be surrounded. That which has seemed so simple, so easy of accomplishment *while you were in class and your attention was upon Us* (for that is *Our feeling* of mastery which We have given you through radiation) then recedes from your outer consciousness—because, by your change of attention, you allow the feelings of depression, doubt, fear and general effluvia of discord (which represents the general consciousness of mankind) to enter again into the subtle essence of your mental body; into the sensitive consciousness of your feeling world; into your etheric body and then into your flesh.

It is My hope and sincere decree that those whose worlds have been accelerated to the point where they *can* grasp and comprehend this Law, may learn that *constant vigilance* is so necessary to enable them to hold the vibrations of their inner and flesh bodies *above* connection with that of the mass mind. I now decree that this shall be so powerfully charged into your outer consciousness that you never again forget it and thus sink back into the inertia which has made you "sleep" for centuries; just accepting the minimum life has to offer; just to keep your bodies alive and your souls nourished to a certain point. Again, *if you will consciously accept it,* I now create around you and your worlds a great oval of pure, blazing white light from My Own heart, which is the vibratory action of My consciousness. This will act for you as a deflector to those currents of discordant energy in which you move in the outer world; which slow down the vibrations of your inner and flesh bodies and again connect you with the mass distresses of mankind.

Law of Life—A Science of Vibration

Beloved friends, as the Great Ones have told you many times, *the action of this Law is mechanical.* It is absolutely and positively a science of vibration. The speed with which the electrons revolve around the central core of each atom in your mind (mental body) is determined by the thoughts you entertain. When those thoughts are of perfection and on the expansion of God's good to His Universe, the vibratory action of the electrons in your mental body is rapid and they deflect the mass thought-forms of destruction which float in the atmosphere of Earth. These are deflected just as a rapidly whirling propeller deflects dust which would otherwise rest upon it. When you allow your mental body to connect with discord, whether it be recorded in newspapers, over the radio, television or in passing conversation, you immediately slow down the vibrations of your electrons. As they slow down, they are more "open", let us say, to the mass accumulations of depression, fear and other negative conditions; which then anchor into your mental body and draw it from the upward course of your aspirations.

The same is true of your emotional bodies. You come into these magnificent classes, sending your love and adoration to the Ascended Masters and other Great Beings in songs and decrees. In this way, you raise your emotional bodies into a more rapid pulsation. The electrons move more rapidly around their central core in the atom and your emotional body is then magnetizing *only that which is good.* As soon as you allow your feelings (emotions) to tie into disapproval, fear, anger or discord of any kind (and the name thereof is "legion"), you slow down the vibrations of those feelings and lower them into the strata where those mass feelings of imperfection abide.

When you endeavor to satisfy the appetites of the four lower bodies by taking into the physical form intoxicating liquors, flesh foods, chemical combinations which do *not* agree with your particular well-being, or taking into the body more substance than it needs to keep it in a healthy condition, fermentation, general disintegration and, finally, "death" ensues. As the electrons move more slowly in their orbit around the central core of the atom, you thus open your flesh bodies to disease. It is just the mechanics of living. The holding of your attention one-pointedly upon the ever-presence of God, together with the assistance of this oval of blazing light which I have established about you today, will enable you to keep your four lower bodies vibrating above the discord in which you move. Then, truly, it can be said that there is nothing in you to which evil and discord can tie!

How think you that the Great Archangel Michael can live twenty hours out of every twenty-four within that substance of the Psychic and Astral Realm and not be touched by it? It is because He keeps the vibratory action of His vehicles whirling at such a tremendous speed that it repels the discord and keeps His world disconnected from the hate creations around those He contacts and desires to set free.

Life So Merciful to New-born

Blessed, beloved ones! Think of the bodies of children when new-born. They come into embodiment with as much of the mercy of the Cosmic Law's goodness as can possibly be allotted to them and this mercy provides for many of them a far better physical vehicle than that to which they would have been entitled otherwise. The vibratory action of the baby body is much more rapid than that of the same body when the soul has used it through a long journey of Earth life. As a rule, especially if there is even a moderate amount of harmony between the parents and among the family in the home, children throw off depression and disease much more easily than do individuals of middle-age or older.

Beloved ones, you who are engaged in this great Endeavor; who have passed through the first fifty years of your life in this embodiment and find it difficult to quicken the rates of vibration of the electrons of your flesh and inner bodies, have just accepted that mass accumulation from the race consciousness. You have just allowed the vibratory action of your physical and inner bodies to "run down" as has the vibratory action of the entire race "run down"—as it passes from youth to maturity and then to "old age".

By the power of the Immortal Three-fold Flame of Life within your own beating heart, *consciously* and *dynamically* draw the Violet Transmuting Flame up through your four lower bodies and up through the atmosphere around you for at least nine feet on every side. This will cause your electrons to be able to spin much more rapidly around their own central core in every atom, because as the Violet Flame passes through your atomic structure, It dissolves and transmutes into light the denser shadowed substance of discord which you have allowed to lodge between the electrons; these shadows actually forming a weight upon them—thus causing them to vibrate more slowly. Do you see? Try to *accept in your feelings* that every cell and organ of your physical body is expressing its Divine Pattern and Plan and refuse to accept "slow death". *Instead, accept and determinedly insist upon* LIFE ETERNAL! It is yours by Divine Right! If you will do this, that which is of shadows will be much more easily dislodged from the atom,—swept into the Violet Flame and be no more.

Your physical form is created by your Body
Elemental, the Devas and Builders of Form and
it is builded around the vibrations of the musical
keynote of your lifestream. As each of the organs
of the body is set into motion, the electrons
(which spin around the central core of the atoms
which comprise those organs) follow the same
rhythm and pattern as your musical keynote.
When one allows the inharmony and discord of
the outer consciousness to break that rhythm and
thus one or more organs is thrown off the natural
harmony of following its keynote, then there
begins the manifestation of disease—discord and
disintegration of the various organs, preceding so-
called "death".

Beloved ones, I come to you today (and
through you to all mankind, for all life is one) to
re-affirm that the vibratory action which makes up
the rhythm of the electrons within the atom *is
under the conscious control of your outer consciousness* which, in turn, should be completely
governed by the "I AM" Presence through the
Holy Christ Self. If you choose to experiment
with this diligently, you will find My words are
Truth.

Elohim of Purity's Part in
The Seven Steps to Precipitation

In the beginning, when the great Helios and
the Beloved Vesta invited the Elohim to create
the planets of our System, Beloved Hercules con-

veyed that invitation to Us and We, individually
as well as in a collective body, said: "We WILL
to render this service". In connection with the
creation of the planet Earth, well do I remember
the time when all of Us were drawn around the
beautiful Being, the Silent Watcher of this planet.
Well do I remember the Flame of Cassiopea which
ILLUMINED to Us the Light Pattern of this
planet, which pattern was held within the Silent
Watcher's bosom, placed there by the Beloved
Helios and Vesta. As We looked upon It, We all
felt the LOVE of Orion and an intensified desire
within Ourselves to co-operate with the God-
parents and bring that planet forth into perfect
form.

Then came My service to life; to hold that
Pattern and Plan inviolate through the Cosmic
Flame of PURITY, so that not one blade of grass,
not one flame-flower should be externalized that
was not a portion of the Divine Idea,—the Pattern
of Perfection as It was held within the bosom of
the Silent Watcher. All through the ages, while
the creation of the Earth was taking place, I held
that Flame and Pattern of PURITY. This, coupled
with the illumined obedience, the sincere humility and the love of the Elohim,—not desiring to
externalize Their Own pattern and form but desiring only to bring forth that which was the
Divine Plan for the Earth,—brought to My heart
happiness indeed.

As you have been told, following My holding

of the Immaculate Concept for the Earth through the use of My Flame of PURITY, My Beloved Brother Vista ("Cyclopea") brought into action His Flame of CONCENTRATION.

Then came Our Beloved Arcturus with His activities of the Seventh Ray—RHYTHM OF IN-VOCATION and the TRANSMUTING POWER OF VIOLET FIRE. The "Seven Steps" were then fully completed by the sealing of the entire creation within the Flame of the Beloved Elohim of PEACE.

Earth Being Redeemed by Calls for Purification from Those Evolving Here

The planet Earth now has fallen far below Its original Divine Design and Pattern which I still guard at Inner Levels *and which shall yet be re-established for the Earth.* Therefore, it brings great happiness and joy to My heart when I see unascended lifestreams willing within themselves to hold up the "cup" of their consciousness and receive again within it even a glimpse of the Pattern of Perfection for this dear Star and for the evolutions upon It (the people of Earth, the Elemental Kingdom and certain of the Angelic Host who volunteered to assist mankind by taking physical embodiment here). It is a joy that I can scarcely put into words to know that, somewhere on this planet Earth, are those who wish to see made manifest the Immaculate Concept for themselves, their fellowman and the planet as well; those who wish to rejoice with the God of all Creation in the perfection of that Divine Design made manifest again.

Then—O, the greatest joy of all—to know that there are those who wish also to use their own energies to help to re-establish that Pattern of Perfection and to bring forth for the Earth and all Its inhabitants the outer manifestation of the Divine Will of the Father. Why would I not rush forward to meet such earnest ones? Why would I not joyously give you, at your call, as much of the power of My Flame as you can accept into your consciousness and show you the perfection which this planet is yet to manifest? Our dear Saint Germain has endeavored for so long to redeem the Earth and make It the planet which shall be called "The Star of Freedom". Then, why would I not bring the vision held in the heart of the Silent Watcher down through the emotional, mental, etheric and physical planes of expression— and lay it before you? To see this Divine Design externalized here again is My reason for being and neither the Other Elohim nor I shall cease to endeavor to assist the Earth and Her evolutions until Our responsibility here is fulfilled. To fulfill it, We require the loving co-operation of unascended beings like yourselves. You are precious, dear and sincere ones who are willing to call forth that Flame of PURITY, the Violet Flame and other activities of the Sacred Fire which can be released from the heart of the Sun to draw the Earth back again into God's perfection.

May I now personally thank you for your endeavors, individual and collective, which have done so much at Inner Levels recently? Above all things, the Beloved Master Morya desires an opportunity to reach the minds of some receptive unascended lifestreams to apprise them of the discordant conditions at Inner Levels of consciousness in the atmopshere of Earth; hoping that some unascended beings, on becoming aware of them, would cooperate with the Ascended Ones to bring such "appearances" back into Divine Order again. Without exception, all of Us are amazed at the loving co-operation which already has been given by you and at the tremendous results (at Inner Levels as well as in the physical appearance world too) which this co-operation has brought about.

Last evening some of Us were looking at the records of the various groups of souls awaiting physical birth for whom you have been calling. We saw there that the number of lifestreams who are to come through physical birth into the world of form this year with more perfect bodies, has been increased from five hundred thousand to one million. *This was brought about just through your endeavors!* The outer mind does not fully cognize what this means to many souls who otherwise might be compelled to go through an entire embodiment with physical, mental and emotional handicaps which I shall not mention.

This subject of birth is so dear to My heart that I have asked for a moment to digress upon it; knowing that, according to your comprehension, you will be willing to assist in the endeavor to give every incoming soul a vehicle of flesh, mind and feelings which can be consciously used by the Holy Christ Self.

Purity—A Delicate Subject to the Human

The subject of PURITY is a delicate one; one from which the human mind cringes and the feelings, in self-righteousness, draw away from discussing. Yet, the vehicles which form the envelopes for the souls who will be the builders of tomorrow are so dependent upon the presence of PURITY at the time of conception, gestation, birth and all through the growing years. Now, in the Name of Mercy, I am going to ask you to call for an Angel Deva of PURITY to be present at every conception which takes place from this moment forth; that Angel to radiate Its feeling and substance of PURITY there, until every one upon the planet Earth and all who wait at the Gates of Birth, have come into the realm of form in dignity, beauty, PURITY and peace!

Conception of a soul to be embodied should take place in thé greatest possible PURITY so that that soul need not be born in the feelings of fear, violence, deceit, rebellion, resentment or in secrecy. It is no small sacrifice for the beautiful

Devas from My Legions to stand in the atmosphere of Earth and perform this service. However, souls conceived and born in the greatest possible PURITY will have better opportunity to hold a connection with the Holy Christ Self *after* birth and the Body Elemental will be able to work more easily with the musical keynote of the lifestream. Then, as the organs and other members of the body are built more strong and perfect, that incoming soul will be able to render greater service to the race.

Beloved ones, PURITY is a matter of *feeling; of consciousness; of radiation!* In days to come, when the atmosphere of Earth and of mankind themselves is much more purified than it is today, the "human veil" will have been lifted and every one will be able to see the causes behind spoken words and actions. *Then there will be revealed those who are pure and those who are not!* Let not self-righteousness, scorn or vows of celibacy fool the man or woman who desires to be *pure in heart.* I am speaking to those who have voluntarily chosen celibacy today because of the need of the hour. Your vows of chastity will bind you throughout this whole embodiment. However, since all life is one, I am speaking through you to all mankind, for We must work with the masses.

You see, you must have a great sense of Divine compassion, understanding and a capacity to pour out the feeling of the Flame of Mercy if you are to raise mankind. I direct your attention to our

Beloved Kwan Yin, the Mother of Mercy, Who spends at least one hour out of every twenty-four calling for and working with those who are outside the pale of legitimacy. I also direct your attention to the Holy Mary—the Mother of the Most Pure,—Who renders a similar service. If, at your call, We can secure the assistance and the presence of the Devas of PURITY in the auras of the parents at the time of conception, (particularly the mothers) as well as the radiation of these pure Beings in the homes where the children are to live, We shall have much greater hope of doubling and tripling the number of more perfect bodies which the Great Law will allow Us to provide for the incoming children in the near future.

*Recent Assistance to Those in "Sleepers' Realm"
and Removal of Discarnates from African
Continent*

Beloved ones, in reference to the "Sleepers' Realm", again—the slower the vibratory action of the consciousness and of the inner vehicles, the more dormant the life and the easier it is for that life to allow itself to enter into that realm of unconsciousness. As the vibration of those etheric bodies is quickened by the pulsations of the Flame of PURITY which you have been calling through these "sleeping" ones—particularly lately —their electrons begin to spin more rapidly and the consciousness again comes to life. In the

Realm of the "Sleepers", many, many more have recently arisen from their couches and have chosen to enter into and become conscious members of the Ascension Temples at Inner Levels. This has been done in these last few weeks, through your calls and through your application.

In the Realm of discarnates and the Earthbound, in Asia alone over one thousand have come forth; in Siberia, ten thousand; in your Western Hemisphere, one thousand.

This morning I am going to ask you to join Me in calls to the Ascension Temple at Luxor (Egypt) for the greatest release of discarnates from Africa that has been known for many ages. Africa—the Dark Continent; Africa—the home of the degenerate races; the greatest concentrate of carnivorous animals and reptiles on the Earth today; Africa—the focus of the greatest psychic and astral creation on our planet at this time!

As the focus for the release of the Transmission Flame during this thirty-day period, the Brotherhood at Luxor (while Their Ascension Flame is more active) will be able to cut many of the discarnates free from Africa, removing at Inner Levels the cause of that which has manifested as voodooism, certain cannibalistic tendencies and various activities with which the average individual is not acquainted. Few unascended beings know what goes on in the heart of those jungles! As the Ascension Temple has asked this morning for your co-operation and assistance; as the Beloved Lord Michael and the Angels of the Blue Flame go into action over Africa and as you now join your voices in song, We are going to endeavor to remove over half a million of these discarnate individuals who really do not belong in Earth's atmosphere. (At this point audience sang: "Purify their Souls, O Flame 'I Am' ").

Dear hearts, as this service is being rendered, around the entire African Continent stand the Legions of Lord Michael with blazing Swords of Blue Flame raised. This is the first time you have been asked to join the ranks of those God-free Legions consciously and become a part of this magnificent endeavor. You will note the lines of force connected with the shadows like a great cloud which forms the astral creation over the African Continent. Now, if you will look upon this with Me, you will see the outline of these figures which represent the souls who have not chosen to let go of their connection with the Earth, These are bound there in the atmosphere because, at some time or other, they have been a part of certain blood-rites and other practices of black magic. As your song has gone forth, the Beloved Lord Michael has chosen to descend so that His feet rest just about ten feet above this cloud.

The distressing conditions which drove into America through the establishment of the slave trade are a part of this which is to be removed this morning in one mighty stroke. The entire Negro population of the Earth will feel the release and

relief as the dissolution of this astral creation
takes place. Those still unascended who, in the
past, were either slave owners or who received
vast money grants through the slave trade, will
feel a certain pressure of energy being drawn out
of their bodies and worlds at this moment. May
I explain here that the "slave trade" does not only
concern that which incorporated the energies of
the American people before the Civil War period,
but I refer also to the slavery all the way back to
Babylon and even before that!

This is the Day of Freedom! In a few moments,
the Lord Michael will suddenly lower His Sword
and, as He does so, every one of His Legions (to
whom We previously referred as having surrounded the entire Continent in this service) will
lower Their Swords at the same time. Just as you
would cut the cables which bind a balloon to
Earth, thus letting it rise into the atmosphere, so
will the lines of force be cut by those swords—
those lines which hold the astral creation in its
present place. As that is being done, one of the
Angelic Beings from Michael's Legions has been
assigned to each discarnate who, when it is cut
free from the mass pressure and pull which holds
it, will instantly "float" right into the arms of this
Being Who will take it from the Earth and into
other Realms which have been prepared for its
purification and instruction. Into Michael's Own
body there will be absorbed and transmuted the
destructive effluvia of this astral creation. It will

be a good picturization for you to watch that inky substance being absorbed into His light through His body and then rush out at the top of His head as a golden pink Flame of loving adoration to God. It is a magnificent thing to see sublimation (refining by fire) through an Archangel.

Now, I believe He signfies that He is ready; so—will you please sing again—this time *to Him*—in order that He may use your energy so released as the authority from the physical octave of Earth which will allow this action to take place as He now lowers His sword. (Audience sang to Archangel Michael). Thank you, beloved children of Earth! In the days that follow, will you try to remember Lord Michael in this act of drawing through Himself the karma of every lifestream who has used the life energies of another through slavery and, in love, transmute it back into a Flame of Adoration to God? When the effluvia of the world is deliberately directed at you, can and will you do likewise? Can you bring back then to your mind the picture of an Archangel so glorious, so beautiful, so majestic and so pure, standing over a Continent filled with such human impurity, and then, in the matter of an instant, drawing these clouds of iniquity through His Own light body, blazing like the Sun at noon-day and making of them music, exquisite color and a paean of praise to the Universal? Now, yours is the same opportunity; the same substance of light. *The same powers of transmutation and sublima-*

tion are available to you! As the violent destructive energies in the atmosphere of Earth swirl backward and forward seeking redemption, the opportunities are numerous for such sublimation by you and, of course, you will gain your own mastery much more quickly by giving such service.

Everyone Deals Only with Impersonal Energy

If you can realize that you only ever deal with *impersonal* energy and if you will stop stamping personality upon it, you will save yourself much agony of feeling and, in dignity, you will be able to transmute and return "Home" whatever clouds of human creation contact or pass through your consciousness. *Within that energy,* spewed forth in hate and in all manner of reviling, *is the pure electron;* is the very body of Myself (pure electronic light), bound in shadows, seeking redemption and freedom. What matters the clothing upon it if it be less than perfection? It is simply something which yet remains to pass through the Sacred Fire of Purification before this Earth can truly be called "The Star of Freedom". While there is yet one unkind thought, feeling, spoken word or deed; while there is yet any impure radiation at all—"Freedom's Star" is not complete.

So, if you should be the recipients of some of that homecoming energy of discord, you can release and redeem that energy through the impersonal dignity of the use of the Violet Transmuting

Flame or the Cosmic Blue Lightning of Cosmic PURITY from My Own Heart. Then that which is driven *toward* you in hate will go forth *from* you in freedom and as a paean of praise to the Universal God. When you do this, you become an Open Door for the redemption of the polluted energies of this planet. *Someone must do it* and that is really what you offered to come into embodiment here to do! It is your reason for being and it is your opportunity to gain your own mastery by rendering a great service of purification to the Earth.

Turning Our attention for a moment to those in what has been called "The Compound", three more of those who yet remained within that darkness have now joined the group which has come forth. Theirs is a most difficult task—in having to daily return into that concentration of hate, after having taken a public stand to accept the Will of God and the assignment of the Karmic Board. Yet, each one of them has gone back for one hour of every day; they have lived up to their vows and that, in itself, is quite miraculous for I need not tell you that all of you within this room have made vows (more than once) that you were not able to keep because of certain frailties of the flesh. However, since they came forth from the "Compound" and bent the knee to the Presence of God, not one of them has refused to return to that "Compound" for one hour out of every twenty-four.

As two results of that, they have three new recruits and even a more magnificent activity can now take place. The Law is now allowing Beloved Lord Michael Himself to enter the "Compound",—not in the blazing light with which you are familiar but, through mercy—clothed from head to foot in deep indigo blue. Even His glorious golden hair is covered with a cowl and only the radiation of His gentlest love silently permeates that atmosphere. Once in every twenty-four hours that Silent Figure passes through the "Compound"; none knowing Who He is. However, before the year is out, you will see a change in the consciousness of those who dwell there; for no one can be exposed to the love of that Being for very long, without *eventually* becoming that love which He is!

I thank you for your attention, and for your love. I am grateful that the Cosmic Law allows Us to give you even a slight glimpse of what your applications are accomplishing and I command that, as you return home and into your own sphere of influence after this meeting today, that My Cosmic Flame of PURITY shall keep accelerating the vibratory action of your thought, feeling, spoken word and deed, your etheric bodies and your flesh until you completely "tune out" of every rate of vibration which would let you accept imperfection again.

Within every electron which is released from the heart of God is the power to create and sus-

*tain the Kingdom of Heaven for yourself, your
family, your world and the students entrusted to
your loving care—right here on Earth.* Within it
is My Flame of PURITY. Right within the
brazier of your heart you carry the most powerful
concentrate of the "Atomic Accelerator" for which
you in this group have been calling for so long.
You have full and free access to all that We are
and all that We have. Today, through the concentration of My Flame of PURITY released from
My Presence with you here, I have washed from
your inner and physical vehicles (bodies) literally
tons of the accumulated atomic consciousness of
impurity and imperfection. Please accept this as
having been done for you—in the Name of God—
and go forward God-pure and God-free!

Remember that the present vibration of your
own atomic consciousness (even though you rail
against it) is more comfortable to you in this
physical appearance world than a more rapid
vibration would be and a tendency to "settle
down" back into that cocoon is ingrained in the
habits of the human race and the feelings of the
outer self. The tendency to lethargically accept
the pattern of imperfection must be guarded
against! You must hold, hold, hold to the power
of God and to PURITY which allows the concept
of your own Divinity to flash through your mind;
to fill your feelings with happiness and ecstasy;
to charge your etheric body with God's pattern

of perfection and to externalize through you as magnificent, useful, vital, living flesh.

I shall watch now and endeavor to help you to hold that light which has been drawn forth about you and help you to sustain it until, after a short interval, Beloved Vista (known to you as Cyclopea) will bring to you the activity of CONCENTRATION which is within His Ray.

Good morning to you and God-blessings from My heart!

Vista

(also known as "Cyclopea")

Beloved Elohim of Fifth Ray

(CONCENTRATION AND CONSECRATION)

Divine Complement— *(Feminine counterpart)*

Crystal

BELOVED CYCLOPEA

O Vista, (Cyclopea), God's All-Seeing-Eye—
    Thy radiant light now floods the Earth from Realms on High.
We love Thee, we bless Thee, Beloved Elohim;
    We now find in mankind some souls through whom we can
        begin
To magnetize and vitalize God's Heavenly Love,
    Released in joy from Mercy's Flame above.
O Elohim of perfect sight and melody—
    O, Vista—Blessed One—We all love Thee.

The perfect eye and perfect ear are Thy design;
    And Thine the power, every hour, these to refine;
The feeling of healing is also Thine to give,—
    Perfection's resurrection now blaze—through all—O make it
        live!
Release, increase acceptance of Thy every gift,
    For such co-operation would all lift.
O make us strong, all free from wrong, supplied by light—
    O Vista dear—*now* help us "make things right!"

Expand it now through every brow, O Vista dear—
    Thy Ray of Green that keeps serene; dissolves all fear.
To others, our brothers, and all that we pass by—
    Blaze to us and through us the comfort that God 's always
        nigh!
Release the Music of the Spheres in sweetest sound,
    That everyone may hear the world around.
Draw all mankind's attention to God's Heavenly Plan
    Held by the Elohim since Earth began.

O Heavenly Friend of Light and Love—make all now free;
    Draw all our Earth and all upon It unto Thee!
It 's thrilling, joy-filling, to hear about Her birth;
    The story of glory—the first creation of our Earth.
Thy oceans bright of Cosmic Light around Her swirled
    Will bring again Perfection to our world.
O Vista, Mighty Elohim! We now implore
    Assistance never come to Earth before!

Gifts from our Sun, Most Holy One, from Earth we call;
    Love's blessings to Thee, Thy Heart-Flame and Elohim all.
Archangels and Masters and Cosmic Beings free,
    World Saviours and Devas,—all Heavenly Hosts now bow
        to Thee!
The Sun God and Sun Goddess of our System dear
    Send Envoys of God's Love to bless Thee here;
Through Helios and Vesta for all Thou hast done—
    All blessings from the Sun behind the Sun!

MELODY: "When Day Is Done" (old song).

110

5

I AM "Vista" (known to you for many years as
. "Cyclopea"), the All-Seeing-Eye of the Eternal
God! I have come this day from the Great Central Sun (the Sun behind the Sun, as It is sometimes called) as a Cosmic Messenger, rendering
the great service which is performed each Christmas Season when the highways between the
Galaxies are opened and the Great Golden Doors
which separate the Solar Systems are swung ajar.
Then, great Beings Who are naturally held by the
cohesion of Divine Love within the orbits of
certain planets are now given freedom to travel
between planets and Systems; thus enjoying the
glory of Cosmic friendship in Universal service.

At the opening of the Feast of Shamballa each
year—at the celebration of the Christ-mass—the
Solar Systems open the Cosmic Highways. May
I explain to you just a little of what this means in

111

relation to your own rather limited knowledge of Science?

The gravity pull of Earth which holds the physical forms of your Evolutions upon the planet during the course of embodiment, also—through magnetic attraction—holds those unascended life-streams who particularly belong to Earth's evolutions, even though not in embodiment at this time. These latter abide in the atmosphere of your Earth at different levels of consciousness. These "levels" are sometimes referred to as the "Inner Realms". Similarly, there is a like power of cohesion which holds within the compass of each Solar System those intelligences, even God-free, Who are rendering service to the Evolutionary Scheme. The Cosmic currents which surge like great tides through the Galaxies so far beyond the comprehension of your finite minds, are very powerful; so much so that even Intelligences of great light might be swept out into a different course from which They began, were They to proceed against the cohesive power which is the governing order of the Galaxy, the Solar System or the Planetary Scheme. So, at the time of the Christ-mass, there is a great Cosmic Dispensation granted and the "King's Highway" (We might say) is opened from the Central Sun to every Sun beneath It in this Galaxy, as well as to Their planets. Certain magnetic currents are then established through those Highways, so that those Intelligences Who wish to travel, may do so in

safety and not be swept into other Cosmic tides.
As these Intelligences are thus enabled to visit
other Stars, Suns and Systems, They associate with
Friends Who are there, some from the Angelic
Kingdom, Ascended Masters and Cosmic Beings.
This also enables such "Travellers" to visit and
participate in the activities of the Ascended Master
Retreats on Earth which are active during this
time, ministering to the unascended evolutions
of our planet. These experiences are the gift of
the Cosmic Christ to These Intelligences Who
serve. Each year, some Being is appointed and
given the opportunity to go from Sun to Sun and
open those Highways with the Cosmic Wand of
Authority. Today, because of the magnetic pull
of your love for Us, your invitation to Us to come
to you here and the tenacity of your natures
(proven through the years of service which tenacity is one of My qualities and part of My nature)
I have been given the opportunity of opening
these highways this year, as Messenger of the King.

Even now, as I stand before you, come the
"Elect" from every System—not all coming to the
Earth, no!—but to visit and enjoy the Sacred
Week of Harvest here and the Holy Days. Along
that pathway come also those Great Ones Who
will enter the Sacred Halls of Shamballa and pay
homage to Sanat Kumara—(blessed be His
precious Name!) and to the Spiritual Hierarchy
Who serve with Him, thanking Them particularly
for the tremendous accomplishments of this year.

Over that Highway will come Cosmic Envoys from other Systems, Who will bring greater assistance for 1955. This could not have been offered were it not for the tremendous manifest works brought about by the willing co-operation of unascended lifestreams and God-free Beings. Through the endeavors of presently incarnated chelas, lifestreams have been released from the "Compound" who have been bound there for millions of years!

Not lightly does the cohesive power of love draw the attention of Cosmic Beings engaged in service of such great import and extent that your sweet minds could not possibly comprehend them at this time! Not lightly was the consciousness of Victory drawn to the Earth by Our Beloved Saint Germain in His desire to give assistance to mankind! Not lightly do the Archangels break the silence of the ages and enable you to give on the written page (as your gift to your fellowman) Their words and some little description of Their activities! Not lightly come the Elohim from the Heart of Celestial Heaven into the atmosphere of Earth, explaining to finite minds the orderly procession of precipitation in creation! Yes, We do love this Earth more than anyone else, except perhaps the Beloved Helios and Vesta, the Seven Archangels and the Silent Watcher, Who holds within Her bosom *even today* the Divine Plan and Immaculate Concept for Our dear Earth.

You see, the Earth was created by Our very life; builded from Our energies and vital force,—for millions of years was Our energy woven into Her rivers and mountains, Her great seas and vast plains. After so many millions of years spent in loving and sustaining this planet, We would not like to see dissolved the handiwork of Our love, just because of the ignorance and shadow-creations of Her evolutions, any more than you would like to see dissolved that to which you had given so much of yourself. So, in part, it is a natural activity for the Elohim to come to Earth again to those who want to transmute the shadows and free this planet, returning Her to the perfection She once knew in the heart and bosom of the Silent Watcher, even before time was!

The Seven Steps to Precipitation

Today, I stood in the atmosphere of Earth and, impersonally looking upon that lovely Silent Watcher, I thought back upon that day when the first call came from the God-parents of Our System (Helios and Vesta) ; when We willed to be a part of Her creation. I thought upon the time when, with Hercules, We said: "Yes, We WILL to serve"; when the great WISDOM (as well as PERCEPTION and ILLUMINATION) of Cassiopea showed us clearly what was to be done; when the LOVE of Orion stirred within Our hearts an intensified willingness to leave Our activities in the Cosmos and, *rhythmically*, give whatever service was required to bring that small but beautiful "jewel" (your Earth) out of the unformed into the formed; when We looked through the Crystal Ray of PURITY and saw the Divine Design and Immaculate Concept of Helios and Vesta for the Earth and Its evolutions. We found that Divine Plan to be good and beautiful and that it would make the Earth a literal "jewel" in the planetary System. Its gifts of light, perfume and music would add to the beauty of the Galaxy—part of the great necklace of the Cosmic Sun of the System. We knew then that it would be Our great joy to create this "jewel" and bring Her to Her greatest perfection, adorning the Solar System.

Then came My activity. I am He Who is known as the Ray of CONCENTRATION. Of course, after My service comes that of My Illustrious Brothers—the Mighty Arcturus of the Seventh Ray (representing RHYTHM OF INVOCATION and TRANSMUTATION BY VIOLET FIRE) and the Elohim of PEACE of the Sixth Ray, Whose service is to seal the finished creation in the protection and perfection of Cosmic Christ PEACE.

Energy Dissipated Without Concentration

What can be accomplished on Earth, even in mundane activities of your daily living, *without CONCENTRATION*—from the smallest task of learning a recipe for your kitchen fare to the greatest dexterity of technique which produces lovely music; to the greatest development of science; to the magnificent perfection of the educator, preacher and statesman? If there is not CONCENTRATION, there is only mediocrity; only the bare surface is scratched. However, those who determine to rise above the masses, take one facet of living and masterfully develop it; deciding within themselves to excel at least along one line of expression. So, they dedicate themselves to this end, consecrating their lives, attention and endeavors, their time and substance; all to achieve this one definite purpose.

According to the CONCENTRATION of those energies is their development; is their mastery; is their efficacy. How often is it said of someone in the world of form that he is "Jack of all trades but master of none!" Looking as I do, both in My capacity as Elohim (the All-Seeing-Eye of God) and My activities with the Karmic Board, I see so much that is just at the point of being precipitated into actual manifestation. Then, suddenly, the CONCENTRATION is dissipated; the attention is drawn away from that which has been deliberately designed and actually begun to be lowered into physical form. Thus the once desired manifestation is abandoned before it can actually appear here.

After We had looked into the beauty and perfection of the Divine Design for this planet through the current and Ray of the Elohim of Purity, what *could* come next but CONCENTRA-

TION,—the drawing of energy and concentrating it around those convex Rays which had been established as the form of the Earth? We had to CONCENTRATE light substance to make the planet solid enough to be able to hold sea, land and general physical form. If We had proceeded through those first four steps (the WILL TO DO; the PERCEPTION as to what should be done; the joy of serving in LOVE; humble enough to do it God's Way—in PURITY) and then had refused to CONCENTRATE upon the task until the planet finally began to revolve upon Its axis; until Virgo and the Beings of Nature had perfected It; until Amaryllis had experimented with nine hundred Springs—what would have happened? *There would have been no Earth!* Yet, even you who are today the maximum development of CONCEN-TRATION in the West (so far as the student body is concerned)—you have only touched the fringe of following things through to manifestation!

It is Law—actual scientific Law—that what you begin *can be accomplished,* when it is in agreement with God's Plan to bring perfection forth; whether it be healing, precipitation, financial freedom, eternal youth, the restoration of a limb—*it can be done*—but the "stick-to-it-iveness" (which is such an important activity of My Ray and the qualification of the energy of My life) is required to produce these.

Greatest Obstacles to Successful Precipitation

Now, what are the obstacles which are encountered in the unascended state that delay your endeavors at instantaneous precipitation? They are mostly discouragement and doubt. When that upon which you work and which comes from the seeming "invisible" does not appear according to the outer mind's reckoning of a time limit, sometimes the project is abandoned just as it is ready to come "through the veil" into the physical appearance world.

I have seen men and women on the verge of great financial mastery, stop working on their project *just within an hour* of receiving their financial freedom! I have seen individuals, working in Retreats, draw currents for healing over quite a period of time. Then, because that healing seemed not to completely manifest quickly enough for them, they wholly abandoned their work *just five minutes short of a Cosmic manifestation!* Often, such a manifestation, if it had been sustained in faith and constancy, would have revealed much Truth to the consciousness of the race as a whole and would have been of great help to them. The "invisible" Realm is almost filled with uncompleted prayers; with beautiful forms which have never been brought into outer manifestation.

How many of you— (*I know,* for I see with the All-Seeing-Eye) —how many of you, just during these addresses, have decided upon some pattern to manifest—have begun to build it—and have already abandoned your project? Those patterns are floating in the Causal Body "forcefield" of this group and will be dissipated because of the lack of your attention which feeds your life into them; unless you pick them up again and either complete them or return them to the unformed, through the etherealizing power of the Violet Transmuting Flame. If *you* do not reclaim them, your pattern may be picked up and completed by some magnetic lifestream in the outer world and *that other individual then will be the beneficiary of all your work!*

Beloved, sometimes people speak of "strokes of luck"—usually great flashes of financial relief and release which they suddenly receive. Sometimes this comes about because—often—another individual has worked for years upon some project, building a momentum of constructively qualified energy thereby, only to suddenly cut the strings and break the line of CONCENTRATION and attention upon his work. This allows that picture (pattern or form) and momentum to be loosed from his consciousness and float away unclaimed into the atmosphere; to be picked up (mentally) by some other lifestream at the last minute of its preparation—just before it physically manifests. *Then that one reaps where someone else has sown!* As a matter of fact, there is a man right here in your City of Philadelphia who utilizes the benefits of this very Law of which I speak and, through it, he reaps where others have sown. In so doing, he breaks no law, because it is like the unclaimed money in many banks which simply lays there, particularly in the Chancery Courts of England. If no one wants it, some alert lifestream might just as well claim it for use.

Concentrate! Follow Through!

I implore you—you who decide upon some pattern and plan of manifestation—*Follow it through! Follow it through! Follow it through!* CONCENTRATE upon your design for precipitation until you have brought it into fulfillment. *Rythmically work upon your project, but not for long hours at a time* so that you become so tense and filled with anxiety that you neutralize your endeavors.

You have been told that, when We created the planets of this System, We came in *rhythm* and it was the power of My Ray of CONCENTRATION which drew and coalesced the actual form of this Earth. After all, what are mankind's bodies but forms of concentrated energy? This energy, as you know, is drawn forth from the heart of your Presence. Once you have determined to bring forth some constructive manifestation, follow through in the Name of God! Follow through in the Name of God! FOLLOW THROUGH IN THE NAME OF GOD! Stop sitting by the wayside resting, when you are on the verge of Victory!

Do you know the CONCENTRATION it takes to bring forth an invention; to bring forth a scientific discovery to the race? Do you know the CONCENTRATION it took to hold the vision for America? Many of you shared that vision and were a part of the "heart-center" which held that vision for the others.

Now, CONCENTRATION and CONSECRA-TION are almost one and the same, beloved ones; because, first of all, whatever you are going to do that will amount to anything *requires the CON-SECRATION of your life* and that you have not understood deeply enough. It is the CONSECRA-TION of all of your energies to the manifestation of something which will give you mastery over this world of form. Do not feel that to desire mastery over financial lack or mastery over appearances of physical distress in the restoration of health— is selfish, because the full-gathered momentum of your mastery becomes your gift to the conscious-ness of the race at large.

So long ago that I can scarcely remember the time, I learned the power of CONCENTRATION which later made it possible for Me to give to you your planet Earth. Who knows but that even within this room today there may be an Elohim for tomorrow's world? I see several for whom it could be possible.

As you are listening to Me today, from Arch-angel Raphael's Kingdom (Whose specialized quality is CONSECRATION), We have con-

nected a beam of energy with that portion of My
Ray which is anchored within the forehead of every
incarnate lifestream on the planet today. This is
the focus in every physical form where the true
inner sight once functioned freely but this *clear*
inner sight has been dimmed by mankind's mis-
use of energy all through the ages; creating shadows in the consciousness by his use of discordantly
qualified thought, feeling, spoken word and deed.
As this shadowed substance increased through
many, many embodiments, it gradually became
what is now known as the "human veil".

This is simply an accumulation of too slowly
vibrating energy which has formed within the
brain structure itself—this denser substance shutting off from physical sight the Presence of the
Cosmic Beings, Ascended Masters, Angels and the
perfection of the Realms which abide above this
physical appearance world. Through this service
which I am rendering here today to you, I am also
endeavoring to clear the inner sight as much as possible, particularly of the "mystic", of the metaphy-
sician and those who have "stepped out" of the consciousness of the masses, desiring a clearer concept of Truth. I am also giving this assistance
today to the great Leaders of the Orthodox channels of religion; endeavoring to give them as much
understanding of the Great Law as is necessary to
convince them that *We are* and that *We are ready
and willing to assist mankind,* by offering the full
power and pressure of Our light and feelings of

Mastery over everything human, thus helping them to find their way back to the complete freedom which God intended them to enjoy from the beginning.

Thank God for His Great Mercies!!!

As some of you know, I am also the Elohim of Music and so My activities and talents are quite diversified. Through the recent release of your marvelous decrees and lovely songs which you have directed right into the "Compound" itself, We now have one hundred fifty individuals who have come out from that unhappy Realm. Personally, I would like to congratulate you on your use of music in this instance and for this purpose, as music does not create the antagonisms in their feelings; which antagonisms I hope you will never have to see! These lifestreams will now enter the Halls of Karma this Saturday evening at the same time the ceremony at Shamballa takes place.

As a result of your service tonight, just as I entered your "forcefield", We received a merciful grant for the benefit of the incoming children. One hundred thousand of those who would otherwise have been blind will be born with sight; fifty thousand of those who would have been deaf, will hear; fifty thousand of those who would not have been able to speak will now have the gift of speech and (almost the greatest of all to Me) — two hundred thousand of those who would have been mentally ill will come into physical birth with their minds balanced and sane. I am so grateful to all who have made this possible! (Audience arose and stood for a few moments in silent gratitude.)

Yearly Informal Gathering at Shamballa

Beloved ones, while you are standing here, the love and light of the King's Highway (now opened), is releasing the gifts of Its light to the Universe. At this time Shamballa's blazing Altar holds upon It the Immortal Three-fold Flame of Life which the Beloved Sanat Kumara has brought here from Venus and sustained by His very life all through the ages. That Great One now walks among His guests, greeting and blessing them. The Masters, too, greet each other and walk arm in arm. Some of them have not seen Their Friends for a very long time, having been engaged in specific services in various places; also the Angels and Devas (in restraint, but yet in great joy) meet and clasp hands . . .

Tonight this is an informal gathering. All of the Great Chohans, all of the Great Masters, all of the Angels connected with Earth's evolutions, look forward all year to this annual return to Shamballa. In a way, it is similar to the way you feel when you are returning home, only much more joyous and glorious because each one knows something of the great welcome He will receive from The King and tonight all are in informal attire. Most of those present are in long, white tunics or tunics of various colors .

The Beloved Lady Venus has come and She and Sanat Kumara have been walking together among the guests. Someone has placed a beautiful lei of flowers around Venus' neck. Beloved Victory is also present. Many of your more recently Ascended Friends are at this gathering tonight, especially all of those from this group here who have Ascended some time since and, when you leave your body tonight while it sleeps, you, too, will come and join Us.

The doors have been opened now to the Great Central Temple wherein abides the Great Sanat Kumara. Those of you who are familiar with the procedure here will remember that a bouquet of the favorite flowers of each Master is precipitated before that One as He or She enters the Temple. This is a personal gift from the Host, Sanat Kumara. So, everyone is adorned with flowers. Some of the Lady Masters wear them in Their hair, if it is piled high upon Their heads or, if the hair is loosely worn, They wear the flowers as a corsage. Some of the Gentlemen wear them in the belt of their magnificent tunics.

All the air is filled with such joy because, as each new-comer enters and sees a Heart-friend, there is a burst of music. This outburst of melody is a natural expression' of their feelings of gratitude for this blessing of renewed friendship. There is that feeling of reunion after having been separated by variations of service in the field for so long. In the background there is soft music playing—instrumental music only. However, in the distance you can hear the happy singing of the Cherubic Choir. Wherever great numbers of the Cherubim are gathered in Cosmic activity (especially at Shamballa) They express Their happiness in song. It is just Their natural expression of joy. You can hear the overtones of that beautiful music in the distance as the Cherubim float in the atmopshere.

Beloved Lord Maitreya is also here tonight in informal attire, wearing golden sandals and the white garment which is deeply embroidered in purple at the bottom and at the cuffs of the sleeves. This color brings out the magnificent violet of His eyes. The eyes of Lord Maitreya are beyond description in their beauty, I think.

To night's activity is preparatory to the great formal ceremony of next Saturday (Transmission of the Flame Activity) —but the Flame is already present upon the Altar and Its radiation is a tremendously vivifying blessing to all. As you look at the festivities and see everyone with happy, smiling faces, you will note that, once in a while, a quiet group will enter who stand by the great pillars and do not seem to mingle with the Guests. These are chelas who have left their physical bodies while they sleep and have been drawn here by directing their attention toward Shamballa before entering sleep, *hoping to get there!* They are a little on the timid side and they stand on the fringe of the activities. However, a little later, they will be approached by one of the Angelic Envoys and drawn into the happiness of the occasion. Later this evening, you too will come to Us in your finer bodies.

Every Guest who enters Shamballa brings Our Beloved Host a personal gift. The harvest of this year's endeavors will be brought to His Altar next Saturday (Transmission night) *but these gifts* of which I now speak are *personal* to Him. Sanat Kumara already has many leis of flowers around His neck; He wears flowers in His hair and carries others. Sanat Kumara is so gracious— He never refuses any gift that is given—however small it may be. From time to time, Beloved Meta (His daughter), Beloved Lady Venus (His Twin-Flame) and some of the Others relieve Him of this "overflow" and They bank them upon a table which is near by. Then, in a moment or two, He is literally covered again with these beautiful expressions of love.

The Archangels and Archaii are here; the Serapic Host in Their great dignity are present also. Beloved Maha Chohan appears with unbound hair tonight. This is most unusual for Him in a public gathering. Pallas Athena (His Twin-Flame) Who usually wears Her hair piled high upon Her head, is wearing it just hanging down

Her back tonight and it is held together at the nape of Her neck by a jewelled barrette.

Now, I am told that Our gathering here will listen if you care to sing your song to Beloved Sanat Kumara and send your love here. This will help you to prepare for the greatest Transmission of the Flame activity this Earth has thus far known. (Group sings to Sanat Kumara)

All of these happy, smiling Friends at Shamballa are now sending their positive, powerful feelings of love to you which I know you do feel. Consciously accept it and ask that it be eternally sustained, all-powerfully active and ever-expanding.

By the way, dear hearts, when Our beloved Guests *come* to Shamballa, They use the music of that lovely melody from Lemuria ("Auld Lang Syne") and when they *leave* Shamballa, they use the melody "God Be With You 'til We Meet Again". You have "tuned in" to this in your selection of the music of that hymn as your closing song in your meetings.

Now, as you move freely about in the heart of Shamballa tonight, tomorrow night and Saturday, you will bring here the harvest of your year's endeavors. Just think how much that is this time— every lifestream incarnating on Earth this year has taken the vow to serve Sanat Kumara; hundreds of the "Sleepers" have arisen from their beds (some of those have been sleeping for cen-

turies) ; thousands of discarnates having been removed from all of the continents; and one hundred fifty of the most difficult of the lifestreams
from the "Compound" are now willing to enter
the Halls of Karma and stand before the Karmic
Board. This is a mighty harvest for which the
Karmic Board *as One* (and I, as Their Spokesman)
give you Their eternal gratitude.

PERSEVERE IN WELL-DOING! You have
proven to Us what *can be done.* This coming year
more children will be born with better bodies—
with limbs that are straight and strong; with eyes
that can see; ears that can hear; lips that can
speak; hands and arms perfect and not withered
and with balanced minds which will be able to
consciously connect with the God-self. Besides all
this, there has been the dissolving of the great
cloud of that shadowed substance over Africa (the
Third Episode of Washington's Vision Itself).
This latest accomplishment took place within the
last two weeks. *O, what a harvest!* No wonder there
come to the Earth *now* Cosmic Envoys from the
Great Central Sun! WEARY NOT IN WELL-
DOING! PERSEVERE! When your manifesta-
tions seem to lag, think of Me and say: "If
Vista had not persevered, my feet would not be
standing on the Earth today—nor could I look at
the blue sky. There would be no America and no
focus on Earth for the Freedom Flame. Vista
had no more with which to work than I have—He·

had only light, CONSECRATION of purpose and CONCENTRATION of energy to *follow through, follow through, follow through to Victory* in God's Name!"

I thank you.

Arcturus

Beloved Elohim of Seventh Ray

(Rhythm of Invocation and Violet Fire)

Divine Complement— *(Feminine counterpart)*

Diana

GREAT ARCTURUS

Great Arcturus, God of splendor;
   Elohim of Violet Fire!
Anchor now Thy victory through us—
   To be like Thee—we aspire.

Violet Fire of God's perfection,
   Dear Arcturus now controls;
Cosmic Flame of Resurrection—
   In Its heart our Earth It holds.

Great Arcturus, for Earth's Victory,
   Now Thy Violet Fire release;
By Thy great transmuting power,
   Change all discord into peace!

Free our Earth and all upon It
   From all never meant to be;
All the Angels, Elementals—
   All on Earth now worship Thee!

God of glory, Light resplendent,
   In Thy radiance let all live;
Through Thy Ray in every forehead—
   Light expand and wrongs forgive!

Thine the power; Thine the glory;
   Thine the Victory—God-success!
We call for Thee and Thy Loved One,
   All God's gifts of happiness.

HYMN TUNE: (First lines)

"Jesus calls us o'er the tumult
Of our life's tempestuous sea . . ."

133

7

I AM the Elohim of INVOCATION and
RHYTHM Who brings to you and all life—
through the use of the Violet Fire—Infinite FREE-
DOM, *when you desire It enough!*

From interstellar space, through all the planets
belonging to this System, I am constantly looking
for those lifestreams who desire FREEDOM—
FREEDOM from illness. limitation and distress
of every kind! Where will you find that FREE-
DOM? Right within your own life! In the beginning of your individualization, God created
your Divine Self-conscious Intelligence—your own
individualized "I Am"—a White Fire Being from
the Universal First Cause, with the capacity to
draw forth from life every God-gift you might
ever require to be able to manifest perfection.
In the great Eternal Scheme of things, I am He
Who answers the call of the heart-beat of any
individual when that heart, *deeply and sincerely*

from within itself, desires to release life which
has become bound; giving it FREEDOM from
disease, from lack, from fear and limitation of
every kind and description. *Within that life
itself* is the fullness—the fullness— *the fullness*
of Almighty God!

This Christmas Class is dedicated entirely *to
the bringing into your feeling worlds the realization that within your own life is every quality
and power* you could ever possibly require to
bring about God-mastery for your self and for
your fellowman.

How I love you—Sons and Daughters of FREE-
DOM! You are those who have chosen to give
of your own life energy, in commanding and
demanding from the Universal Law, gifts, powers
and blessings for this recalcitrant race; for this
Earth which We originally created in such perfection; which We designed in such love; which
We fed with such constancy and which has fallen
into such shadows that It actually groans as it
turns heavily upon Its axis.

Life (which is light-essence) quiescent, contains
within Itself *all the power* of the Universal First
Cause which created the System, the Galaxy and
the entire Universe to which you belong. This
same life (light) flows from the heart of the Great
Central Sun through your own White Fire Being;
then through your "I Am" Presence into and
through your physical heart, animating your world.
Within that light, beloved ones, is anything and

everything that you require! From that same primal life and light We created the planet on which
you presently abide; as well as all the planets of
this System. From that light do Helios and Vesta
give to you the radiation of the Sun in the
Heavens. From that same life has the Beloved
Jesus given you the miracles, marvels and mastery which mankind recognizes with more than
ordinary feeling of gratitude at the Christmas
Season.

Develop Your Own God-qualities from Within

Today, I urge you with all the intensity and
pressure of My Being, to *develop your life*—
develop the qualities of perfection which are
within it. Call forth what you wish from the
heart of that life which flows from the Universal
and call to Me, if you wish to release into outer
manifestation from within your own life, whatever powers, qualities, gifts and activities are required to perfect your own individual world and
that of your fellowman. Wherever there is one
lifestream who sincerely desires FREEDOM and
in constant RHYTHM *invokes and commands
it,* there shall I be to give that one assistance until
that FREEDOM is physically manifest.

In the drawing forth and developing of Our
Solar System, the Seven Elohim (Who are the
Builders of Creation) are well qualified to bring
to you an understanding of the *conscious power*

of Precipitation. Today, through this magnificent "forcefield", We are writing upon your life consciousness with the energy of Our feelings; giving you an explanation of the very activities in which We engaged while drawing forth this Universe from primal light. You, in turn, may give this gift to mankind. The radiation, power and powers of the Seven Elohim and the constant application of the Seven Steps to Precipitation (if rhythmically and conscientiously called forth) will bring the lifestreams on this planet to mastery in the Power of Precipitation. We cannot urge you too strongly to *follow through* with the concentration upon the pattern you desire to manifest; to contemplate that pattern in its completeness and then to practice, *practice, practice* until that precipitation, following along through the "steps" We have given you, is made physically manifest—outpictured as the perfection of the design which you have been holding in your mind.

Seven Steps to Precipitation

Let Me review again the activities of the Elohim so that I may show you where My part in the Cosmic building fits in.

First: The Mighty Hercules' WILL TO DO (DECISION). Nothing ever can be accomplished here or anywhere else until the lifestream (ascended or unascended) wills within itself to do; to act; to co-operate with some portion of the God-intelligence.

SECOND: Then comes the quality of Cassiopea, with His power of PERCEPTION (ILLUMINA-TION), showing one the perfect thing to do; getting the clear picture of the pattern or design to be precipitated.

THIRD: Next comes the LOVE of the Mighty Orion, holding constantly to the original pattern and vision of perfection and feeding the feelings of Divine LOVE and light into it, until the complete manifestation appears.

FOURTH: Then comes the PURITY of Beloved Claire (Elohim of Purity), holding the perfect pattern steady and unchanged; holding to the purity and symmetry of the original design.

FIFTH: Then comes the quality of Vista— CONCENTRATION (and CONSECRATION) —the power to stay with one pattern and one idea until it is lowered into form, instead of letting the mind flit from one design to another; for, *in such procedure, nothing at all is made manifest.* You see, it is in the following through with the mathematical Science of Precipitation that you gain mastery and results.

SIXTH: As Our Beloved Brother, the Elohim of Peace, serves life upon the Sixth Ray, ordinarily His activities would come next. However, in the activities of Precipitation, although I work upon the Seventh Ray, My quality of INVOCA-

TION IN RHYTHM comes next and takes sixth
place here; and the

SEVENTH: is the sealing of the entire manifestation in the feelings of GOD-PEACE from the
Elohim of Peace Himself. So far as the power of
Precipitation is concerned, the activities of Our
two Rays are inverted.

Rhythm of Application—So Very Essential

As I stated above, My specific contribution to
the building of form is the activity of INVOCA-
TION IN RHYTHM; of the constant feeding of
the desired form to be out-pictured with life
energy, until it is not only a manifest thing but
symmetrically perfect as well. You see, *the constancy of RHYTHM gives symmetry to the form
to be manifest.* RHYTHM and constancy of
application are absolutely essential to bring about
the manifestation of your desired design.

If you will observe Nature, you will easily
recognize the absolute RHYTHM by which all
creation takes place; the rising and setting of the
Sun; the incoming and outgoing of the tides; the
re-current seasons—all in an absolute and perfect
RHYTHM. Those of you who have any practical
knowledge of the value of rhythmic, deep breathing, will understand that, in the balanced
RHYTHM produced in the four lower bodies by
the use of the deep and majestic breath, there
could be no inharmony remain in your feeling

world for any length of time. For those who are subject to the expression of violent emotions, I can but recommend the practice of deep and *rhythmic* breathing; for you will find it an impossibility to stay in a state of discordant agitation if you will use the deep and *rhythmic* breath— *feeling that you breathe the breath of the Almighty Creator Himself.* This slows down those agitated vibrations of the surging sea of emotion.

In the early Golden Ages, beloved ones, when the Archangels and the Ascended Masters *just naturally* walked and talked with unacsended mankind, the magnificent perfection which was drawn forth by the power of INVOCATION was brought about because of the understanding of the necessity for RHYTHM OF INVOCATION and application. This was necessary in order to have a constancy of outflow of the energy from above. This constancy of the release of perfection called forth from the God-head made it possible for the atmosphere of Earth to be kept completely free from disease, disintegration and all manner of human shadow.

In the world of form, mankind pays fairly regular attention to the RHYTHM of feeding the body; to the RHYTHM of doing that which affects the comfort of the outer self; but, in the most important of all— his spiritual activities— RHYTHM is pretty thoroughly forgotten! The science of constancy of prayer and application is seldom seen. However, to draw forth a sus-

tained, visible Flame into the physical appearance
world from the Inner Realms, would require a
sanctified, consciously dedicated and consecrated
group of lifestreams who, rhythmically, at a certain
given hour, repeated day after day, would draw
forth by decree and invocation that mighty concentrate from whence the Flame would burst forth
into visibility.

It is the same with your *individual* application.
If you were to observe a certain RHYTHM and
make your application (your individual calls) at
the same hour every day, you would draw a much
greater concentrate of power and quicker accomplishment than you do when you make your
application fit into the free hours which each day
may choose to give you. It is the RHYTHM of
the "mass" of the Catholic Church and the
RHYTHM of the various Christian religious
services all through the centuries which has held
the power of the Christian Dispensation thus far.
When you observe that same RHYTHM in your
working hours; your time for sleep; your time
for relaxation—holding to that symmetry which
Nature has given you (eight hours for service,
eight hours for sleep, eight hours for relaxation) —
you will have greater harmony in your feelings;
better health in your bodies; and you will be
able to draw forth from within your own life
much greater perfection than you can in spasmodic
endeavors at either work or play.

In the creation of this planet Earth, it was the

joyous, willing desire of *all* of the Elohim to come
together *rhythmically* at a given time—for the time
being forgetting, mind you, all of the activities in
which Their consciousnesses were engaged in the
creation of other planets in other Systems or
Galaxies. They poured Their life into the design
given Them by Beloved Helios and Vesta until
the planet was completed. It was that unbroken
RHYTHM of application on Their part which
made the Earth so perfect in Its symmetry and
design; so beautiful and shining in Its essence and
so magnificent a place for mankind to be able to
take embodiment.

"Keep On Keeping On"

You see, nothing but your own "giving up"—
abandoning your project before it is completed—
can possibly prevent your eventual precipitation.
When once the RHYTHM has been established,
stay with your pattern until the energy required
flows into it, in *rhythmic* release!

Throughout the ages, mankind (even spiritually
inclined souls with great light) , for some reason or
other, refuse to accept the truth that—*if you follow through with precision* the seven "steps"
(powers) of the Elohim in creation—*you must
have manifestation;* that is, of course, unless you
stop your RHYTHM before manifestation appears! If We had ceased Our activities even *one
hour before* the Earth was completed, all of Our

work of such a long time would have been in vain
(and I shall not tell you just how long We gave
Our service to the creation of this planet). Also,
had We discontinued Our RHYTHM before the
Earth's completion, the planet would have begun
to disintegrate and return to the unformed. We
continued and continued — RHYTHM after
RHYTHM—making no mental note at all of just
how long it would take. We just came back again
and again, *rhythmically* pouring Our light, love
and visualizations of perfection, even if it were to
take the rest of eternity! *We just loved that which
We were doing.* Then, one day, I remember it so
clearly—IT WAS COMPLETED! The Earth
began to revolve on Her axis and We heard the
words: "It is finished"!

So it is the same in every application—from the
smallest personal thing with which you may desire
to experiment in precipitation in your home life,
to the greatest Cosmic endeavor which may take
in the evolution of an entire Galaxy. If you will
"keep on keeping on",— observing the Laws from
the Spiritual Octaves as They have been given to
Us and as We now give them to you, *you must
have manifestation!* We will help you if you
wish Us to do so. *Make your call to Us and We
will answer you!* Then, when your precipitation
lies visible and tangible within your hands or
stands completed before you, will you know that
it did not come to you by happenstance and that

it is not just a gift of faith. You will know that it is a precipitation direct from the Universal.

Let us here again consider those "Seven Steps":

First: There must come your WILL (DECISION) to have it;

Second: There must come your PERCEPTION (ILLUMINATION) of what you wish to precipitate;

Third: You must LOVE to create it;

Fourth: You must have PURITY of consciousness to hold your pattern untouched by any imperfection or the changing of its design;

Fifth: There must be CONCENTRATION upon your original design;

Seventh: There must be RHYTHM of application in decree and silent mental thought-force; and

Sixth: Your feeling of God-PEACE must case it around to hold its perfection protected and sustained. Call to the Elohim of Peace to so seal your manifestation in His Flame of Cosmic Christ Peace, that disintegration never touches it and until such time as it has completed the service for which it was created.

When any form has completed its blessing to this world and thereby served its purpose, the process of Etherealization is the dignified way for it to be disintegrated and its component parts return to the Universal from whence it came,— not through the processes of decay and fermentation. That substance should be released as We do

it in Our Octave, through the direction into it of
the Freedom Flame (Violet Transmuting Flame)
in gratitude for Its service. As the Violet Fire is
projected into the heart of the manifestation to be
released, the magnetic pull upon the electrons
which have been held there releases and the
electrons return to the Sun for re-polarization. So
should all things of this world be sent back to the
Universal First Cause when they have completed
the service for which they were originally brought
into being.

Explanation of Violet Fire

Although, of course, the power of INVOCA-
TION may be used to draw forth any God-virtue
and blessing for the benefaction of the race, I am
primarily stationed, spiritual speaking, at the apex
of the Seventh Ray—drawing forth and directing
the Violet Ray and Flame to every Sphere; as well
as into every consciousness which requires purification and sublimation (refining by fire).

Much more will be learned about the Violet Ray
and Flame by the people of Earth in the near
future. Its *main* purpose and use on this planet
is to purify energy which has been discordantly
qualified through the use of the free-will of self-
conscious intelligences. Such purification raises
the vibrations of the energy concerned, returning
it to its original light-essence. Then that same
energy may be requalified and used again to pro-

duce and express perfection in some form. The use of the Violet Flame as a purifying and sublimating agent is required only where distortion of form has resulted through imperfect experimentation with the powers of creation; or where form has served the purpose and use for which it was originally made manifest. Elsewhere, the Violet Ray and Flame can and do render a different service from that which they give to the Earth but this is not of particular interest or use to the people of this planet at this time.

The Violet Ray and Flame are activities of the Sacred Fire. They are energy specifically qualified by Divine Beings to act in the world and experience of any and all who will accept and use Them to purify and return to its original perfection, the energy which is now imprisoned here in discordant mis-creations of the past. The Violet Flame has been feared by mankind because the mis-qualified energy which surrounds them does not like the thought of purification or change. Thus, until very recently, Its knowledge and use was not given to students outside of an Ascended Masters' Retreat, where the positive radiation of the Ascended Master could hold such fear in check until the student felt the confidence, comfort and efficacy of the use of that Violet Fire.

The present Chohan of the Seventh Ray (the Ascended Master Saint Germain) is the Representative of this Violet Ray and Flame to the Earth for the next Cosmic Cycle of 2000 years. When He can secure the *full acceptance* in the *feelings* of the students of the reality and efficacy of Its use, the Earth's redemption will be greatly accelerated.

Saint Germain, Zadkiel (Archangel of the Violet Fire), Holy Amethyst (Twin-Flame of Beloved Zadkiel) and Myself (Elohim of Violet Fire) are all serving together without cessation at this time, to bring the knowledge and conscious use of the Violet Fire to the outer consciousness of those of mankind who are interested in the planetary cleansing and redemption of the Earth *now*.

In this connection, of course, the first step is to get the student to accept *even intellectually* the reality of the Violet Ray and Flame; as well as the reality of the mighty Beings Who wield Its powers at Inner Levels.

The next step is to encourage the student to consciously use the Violet Flame individually and, collectively in groups, until they actually *feel* and *see* its efficacy in their own worlds, as well as on a planetary scale.

To this end I am dedicated. Call to Me and let Me show you how comfortable, how relaxing, how practically efficacious this Violet Ray and Flame can be to you now.

At Inner Levels, unascended beings are offered the knowledge and conscious use of the Violet Flame when they profess a desire to want to progress upon life's pathway and are shown the accumulation of discordantly qualified energy of

their own life essence which prevents further
progress until such substance is transmuted into
light. This purification (which is a self-conscious
application of the individual's own lifestream) has
been referred to by the Church as "Purgatory",
which simply means "a place of purging or purification". However, this idea has been confused
with the "Flames of Hell" and unfortunately, this
distortion of the Truth has created even greater
fear in the souls of men. Where it is recorded in
the Bible that the Earth will be consumed by fire
in the "latter days", it is merely meant to signify
that the Violet Flame will be used to transmute
all imperfection in the Earth, on the Earth and
in Its atmosphere.

When consciously called into action, the Violet
Ray is directed downward by the Being in charge
thereof and, as the student accepts and uses It, It
blazes up in through and around him as a living
Flame of Divine Love, Forgiveness and Mercy;
cleansing not only his physical imperfections, but
also the impurities in the etheric, mental and
emotional bodies.

Use of Violet Flame

To use this Flame, visualize the clearest, most
beautiful, brilliant shade of violet you can. See,
as well as feel It, blazing up, in, through and around
you. To intensify the power of this Flame through
your world, picture it deeper and deeper in color

until you have a brilliant, deep purple Flame. Its
faithful use will bring you peace. Rejoice in the
mercy of Its presence and Its willingness to set
you free. *Let go* of your distresses, known and
unknown and *see just what the Violet Flame can
and will do for you!* I CHALLENGE YOU!
USE IT! WE SHALL HELP YOU!

You already have released in printed form for
the blessing of all who care to benefit by it, the
book containing the addresses of the Seven Archangels, which book brings Their feelings of victorious accomplishment to you. Now We bring
to you Our loving instruction on the concentrated
power of Precipitation and, with the coming of
Our Beloved Elohim of Peace, Who will give the
final address in Our present series, you will have
had charged into your etheric bodies, your minds
and your feeling worlds, some of Our consciousness
of these "Seven Steps to Precipitation"; at least
as much as you are able to receive at this time.

I expect you to follow through these steps of the
activities of Precipitation and, one day, standing
before Me with your perfect precipitation completed, say: "Master, here is one of the results of
the instruction You have given me". I expect this
of you because you are men and women who love
FREEDOM; who are consecrated to FREEDOM.
You have said so many times yourselves—"I am a
son (or a daughter) of FREEDOM". By that very
statement you have bound yourselves to My heart.
You have become part of My world and I shall

not rest until you have freed from within your
own life and fully expressed the perfection of
your own God-quality (the purpose for which you
came into being) and until there have been drawn
forth into, through and around this dear Earth all
the God-powers which are required to re-establish
perfection upon this planet. When We look upon
the face of this sweet Earth and see what destruction has been brought about upon Her—what a
pity! What a shame! Yet, at the same time, We
are so grateful that even a "handful" of people
among all mankind care enough about Her plight
to want to restore Her to Her pristine perfection
again.

At a Great Cosmic Council sometime ago, the
Beloved Virgo (the Being known to you as
"Mother Earth") stood alone before the Great
Karmic Board and as She did, every Ascended
Master and Great Cosmic Being present knelt
before Her in loving gratitude and adoration for
Her patience, love and spiritual hospitality to a
race which even the Karmic Board Itself had decided could not survive. Beloved ones, among
those present, there stood unascended beings—
your dear selves—with your faces shining; your
hearts dedicated; your spirits alive with the love
for the Earth and even the Karmic Board were
stirred deeply. This enabled dispensations to be
given for the Earth which would delight your
hearts—dispensations to give this planet and Her
people more freedom.

I am told that you wish your complete freedom from those "seven mortal sins" which have become rooted in the consciousness of mankind. Do you? (Audience rises) Thank you! Now, in the Name of Almighty God; in the Name of the Seven Mighty Elohim of Creation; in the Name of the Seven Archangels and Their Archaii; in the Name of the Seven Chohans of the Seven Rays and All Who serve with Us— I AM that Freedom! I AM that Freedom! I AM that Freedom! from those activities which represent the sins of men, for these here assembled and all who will call to Me in the future. In the Name of God, I command those sins to LET GO! LET GO! LET GO! LET GO! LET GO! LET GO! LET GO! and IT IS DONE! IT IS DONE! IT IS DONE! *Consciously accept this done now for you*—with full power! Thank you and Good morning!

𝔈𝔩𝔬𝔥𝔦𝔪 𝔬𝔣 𝔓𝔢𝔞𝔠𝔢

("Tranquility")

Beloved Elohim of the Sixth Ray

(Sustained Peace; Ministration)

Divine Complement— (*Feminine counterpart*)

𝔓𝔞𝔠𝔦𝔣𝔦𝔠𝔞

BELOVED ELOHIM OF PEACE

Elohim of Peace! in God's glorious Name—
    We call forth oceans of Thy Golden Flame;
Flame from the Heart of the Great Central Sun;
    Guarded, expanded by Thee, Holy One!
Great is Thy wisdom, Thy love and Thy might;
    Heavenly glory floods forth on Thy light;
Harmony, healing, beauty to bring—
    To Thee we joyously sing!

Peace is the healing of every distress;
    Peace is the feeling of God-happiness;
Peace is the power of all God-control;
    Peace every hour will Victory hold!
Peace is Love's gift to the children of men;
    Peace is forgiveness—again and again;
Peace in the heart, the soul, and the mind—
    Peace fulfills God's great Design!

Elohim of Peace, to Thee ourselves we give!
    In Thy full glory fore'er let us live;
Now take possession, command and control,—
    Over our worlds Thy dominion now hold!
Seal our sweet Earth in Thy radiance, too;
    Rule all Her people in all that they do;
Make them the glory of Freedom's Heart;
    They are of your world a part.

Glory of all our great Universe dear,
    Great Central Sun, we call all Thy love here!
Flood it around our dear Elohim of Peace;
    Make all His power and glory increase.
Bless His Beloved with heavenly grace;
    Let Their great glory, combined, fill all space.
Let all that lives now bless Thee dear One,—
    We love Thee—Great Central Sun!

MELODY: Original, (*Now available on musical recording*)

6

*B*ELOVED children of the One Living God! I come to you today to bring the description of the activities of My Ray (Sixth Ray) —MIN-ISTRATION and PEACE. This now completes the instruction of the Seven Mighty Elohim of Creation on Their Seven-fold Flame in this series of addresses which began some weeks ago. "The Seven Steps to Precipitation" are the unalterable process of all God-creation—finite and infinite.

I come into Earth's atmosphere today through your magnetic "forcefield", the center of which is above your Sanctuary; the energies of which "forcefield" have been drawn here from the heart of Creation in answer to the calls of your precious hearts all through the years. On the energies of your own life I shall write the words which complete the pattern of *conscious precipitation,* by which We created the Universe under the direc-

154

tion of Helios and Vesta. A part of this Creative
Scheme which We brought forth into manifestation at that time was your own sweet Earth, which
is now the platform beneath your feet and has
provided for you and your fellowman a "schoolroom" to which you voluntarily chose to come to
learn the conscious control and mastery of energy.

What We have done on a Universal scale by
the use of these seven progressive "steps" in consciousness, *each and every one of you can and
one day must—use* to draw forth direct from the
Universal those gifts of light's perfection which
are the Will of God for you to enjoy and be able
to give to your fellowman. This is because *the
ability to precipitate is a natural attribute and
power of your own "I AM" Presence*—your Father-
Mother God—the Source of your being and the
creative heart-center of your present consciousness.

Your "I Am" Presence first became conscious of
Itself as a living, breathing Being, when It was
first directed out of the Universal First Cause.
When that Presence found Iself to be an individualization of God-consciousness, It then chose
to draw to Itself the substance of primal light
(life) and qualified it with the God-ideas of Its
Own personal consciousness. This qualified light
was then sent forth by It to create and expand
the beauty, glory and ecstacy of creation.

Since the very nature of God—light—is to expand perfection, that "I Am" consciousness then
determined within Itself to leave for a time the

heart-center of the atmosphere of Its Creator and explore the Seven Spheres of Consciousness which surround Its God-head—the Sun from whence It came. It remained for as long as It chose in each Sphere, to learn to use the specific powers of creation in each of these Realms. In this way, the "I Am" Presence drew into Its Own Causal Body* the seven different momentums of qualified energy which appear as the seven colors around the Upper Figure on your Chart. As the "I Am" consciousness gradually proceeded from Sphere to Sphere, It finally chose the activities of one of those Spheres which most appealed to Its liking and It there decided to develop some specific expression of God-power along one of the Seven Rays which would be Its gift to the Universe.

Creative Experimentation Begins

After this individualization of your own life-stream had passed through all of the Seven Spheres of creative consciousness (the Causal Body of the God-head) those who decided to try embodiment upon the planet Earth then applied for such permission to the Manu of the First Root Race (the Cosmic Being Who was in charge of the evolutions here at that time). Thus, in the denser substance of the Earth-plane, that Presence learned to wield the powers of thought, feeling, spoken

---

* NOTE: For explanation of Causal Body see "The Bridge to Freedom" Vol. 5, No. 6: Pg. 21).

word and action and consciously create as the
Father does. "Hitherto hath the Father worked;
now, the Father and I work"! Now comes the
time when each individualized God-flame of His
consciousness *must work co-operatively with* the
Father to expand the borders of His Kingdom.
The above statement of Jesus has been spoken
by Us to the chelas this year perhaps more than
any other and every man has interpreted it according to his own understanding. Some feel that it
means but a greater radiation of sustained harmony; others feel that it means the spreading of
the Light and Truth by contacting more of mankind, acquainting them with the Laws of Life—
helping to bring them to a realization of the
power and powers of creation *which are within
them.* Still others feel that it is learning the way
and means of actually engaging the energies of
the inner and physical bodies in creating as the
Seven Mighty Elohim create—in a conscious, or-
dered, scientific precision, by the use of thought,
feeling, spoken word and action—thus producing
instantaneous precipitation direct from the Universal.

Of course, "expanding the borders of the Kingdom" *means all of these things—and more!* Now
and then, one will find a naturally peaceful and
harmonious type of individual—the very radiation of whose aura brings the benediction of God's
PEACE to all the life it contacts. Such an one
may be compared to a beautiful flower growing

in a lovely garden, adding to the beauty and perfection of that garden for any and all to enjoy.
However, such a flower is not endowed with the
God-gift of free-will and choice and has no conscious volition or capacity of its own to be other
than it is. It has to depend upon the gardener
for its sustenance and protection and is wholly subject to the caprice of anyone passing through that
garden who might wish to cut it down.

Now, however, you who have chosen to accept
the instruction of the Elohim, as well as the instruction which has been brought to you by the
Ascended Master Saint Germain and the Hierarchy, are no longer to be considered *"uncon-
scious"* radiating centers of Divine Love and
Harmony, no matter how beautiful such radiation may be. At this time, We are seeking those
who are willing to be *conscious* co-workers with
the Spiritual Hierarchy, of which the Ascended
Masters and Cosmic Beings (Whom you love and
worship, at least to some degree) are active Members.

Those among you who can grasp the explanation and use of the Power of Precipitation (which
instruction has now been given you by the Elohimic Builders) *can—and We expect you to—
become masters* of the descent of energy into the
world of form as whatever substance and quality
you require to manifest here; sustaining, protecting and expanding the radiation of perfection for
yourself and your fellowman. Your conscious use

of these powers will more quickly bring this world back again into the Paradise of loveliness which It was in the beginning when It first came forth as Our loving handiwork. Then, one must also become Master of the Power of Etherialization (the instantaneous returning of form back into the Universal when such precipitated form has served its purpose), so that that God-life does not remain imprisoned in any vehicle of expression longer than that prescribed by its Creator for its actual service.

Peace—God's Positive Power

As I speak to you this morning, I shall endeavor at least to touch upon the high points of the assignments which have been given Me to bring to your attention in the limited time which has been allowed Us for this purpose.

First of all, right here,—I would like to remove from your minds the erroneous human concepts concerning the God-quality of PEACE. PEACE is not a negative quality! It is the most positive and most concentrated activity of power which is manifest in any Realm. PEACE is not lethargic, indifferent or inactive! Let us examine PEACE for just a moment as a quality. Just *how much power of control does it require* for you to HOLD YOUR PEACE—to remain absolutely poised and Master of every situation—*regardless of the aggravation*—in the midst of your immediate family,

your business associates, your co-workers in this
Activity or the world at large? You know that
it requires all the power of control you are able
to manifest!

In this series of the explanation of the precipitating activities of the Seven Elohim, I am
the last One to come to you, inverting the posi-
tions of Beloved Arcturus (Elohim of the Seventh
Ray) and My humble Presence as the Elohim of
the Sixth Ray. This is because, after you have
fed the form you wish to precipitate with your
own life and the actual manifestation of that
which you desire has appeared here, that manifestation must then be held within the *feeling* of
undisturbed PEACE; otherwise it will disintegrate
and return to the Universal from whence it was
originally drawn.

When the Ascended Master uses the Power of
Precipitation, He always has a very definite design
in mind which He desires to bring forth
for some specific purpose that will benefit, not
only one lifestream or even a group, but all life
everywhere! He first decides within Himself by
His Own designing power of thought and feeling,
that which He wishes to manifest, even as you
might desire to create one of these lovely ceramic
vases. Then, by projecting forth His feeling of
Divine Love, He calls to Him Elemental life in
the form of electronic light-essence (which fills
the Universe everywhere) and, through the magnetic power of that love, such Elemental life

obeys His request to fill the form He is creating.
The Master then breathes the light and love of
His heart upon that design and, with the feeling
of loving gratitude for the obedience that substance has given Him, He commands that it be
sustained in that form for a certain period of
time; for as long as it can render constructive
service to life.

Divine Economy

Beloved ones, the Ascended Masters are most
conservative in Their use of life. There is a
great Divine Economy of the Cosmic Law which
most generously provides the limitless abundance
of every good thing *for all to use as freely as the
air they breathe* and yet *does not permit the
wasting of a single electron;* nor the sustaining
of a single electron in any form which has served
its intended purpose! The Ascended Masters,
having become the Cosmic Law in action, do not
have any "clutter" in Their worlds or activities.
They know that primal life which comes from the
heart of God must obey Them, because such is
the Law. Therefore, They know that Their
creations, made up of that light, will remain intact
for just so long as They decree it.

Should the Ascended Masters require homes,
clothing, means of conveyance—*anything* They
might require, either in the Realms of Light or
here, when They are assisting mankind—all is de-

signed and precipitated instantaneously from Universal light and serves Their purpose for as long as They desire it. Then, as Beloved Arcturus said in His address, when the form is no longer desired, the directed light Rays of Violet Fire from Their hearts, throats and foreheads enter into the center of that manifested form, releasing the cohesive power from within that precipitation. Then that Elemental life, no longer feeling the cohesive "pull" of that love and command of the Immortal Flame within the form, begins to disintegrate it and automatically returns it to the Sun from whence it came, for re-polarization. Sometimes this Etherialization is *instantly* done, in what would seem to be like a Cosmic "explosion"; sometimes it is done slowly and gradually, just as the petals fall from a flower and its form ceases to be.

So, these powers of Precipitation and Etherialization are now available to you for your joyous, individual use and you are now at a place on the Spiritual Path where you should be using them. *You can,* most assuredly, if you will definitely determine to follow through the concise "steps" which have been given you in Our addresses— *for these "steps" are absolutely mathematical in their precision!*

Allow Me, if you will please, to be somewhat repetitious in bringing again to your conscious minds the consecutive activities of the Elohim as They used the Powers of Precipitation and

Etherialization, which "steps" are unalterably required for the manifestation of any form—from the smallest to the greatest creations.

Seven Steps to Precipitation

First: Nothing is ever created in this world and nothing is ever accomplished along any line until you WILL within yourself to do it! This is the activity of Beloved Hercules and the First Ray. Whether you WILL to walk down the street; to attend a class; to give some service to another; to precipitate a small ring or a large building,— you must first—within yourself—WILL to take the vital energies of your life and accomplish some constructive purpose with them.

Second: This comes under the radiation of the Beloved Cassiopea. After you have willed to create a definite form, one should then ask for the DIVINE PERCEPTION (ILLUMINATION) as to how best to produce that form or, after you have abstractly willed to serve in some way, the PERCEPTION of the Gold Ray is necessary to enable you, through the use of discrimination *and the use of just plain common sense,* to know just what momentums of already developed God-qualities you have to offer and how they will allow you best to serve. Particularly since the time and work of Madame Blavatsky up to the present day, We have had many men and women who have willed to serve the Masters but who indiscrimi-

nately rush forth into action without discreation or
the measuring of their own talents and capacities—
regardless of the type and amount of qualified substance in their worlds which would allow the best
service to be given; also as to how the service
they desire to give might fit into the great Universal scheme. So, after you WILL TO DO, then
you require PERCEPTION to let you know at
least something of that which you wish to do and
how that which your world has to offer will be
able to lovingly co-operate with God's Divine
Plan.

Third: Now comes the step which involves releasing the feeling of DIVINE LOVE from your
heart and this "step" is under the direction of
Beloved Orion. That which you do in service
for the Master or in the use of the Power of
Precipitation, requires the loving co-operation of
all your bodies, *including the outer physical form.*
You have heard it said so often by many of your
great Teachers that, what is done in a sense of
"duty", must be done all over again *in a feeling
of* LOVE. Therefore, you must develop the qualities of feeling of Our Beloved Orion—the loving
constancy of staying with your endeavor until
it is completed; working with it in gratitude, happiness and devotion, with no thought of time,
recompense or personal recognition of any kind;
just serving for the joy of it! That is the activity
of the Third Ray—one of the most important of
"The Seven Steps".

Fourth: Beloved Claire (Elohim of Purity) takes fourth place in precipitating. This means staying right with the PURITY of the original design which has been given into your mind by your own Holy Christ Self at your request; or, if you are among the more fortunate ones who are further developed—directed into your mind by some Master Himself. To hold the PURITY of your design means that you do not personally elaborate upon it, "embroidering" it, so to speak; fitting that design into your own reason, logic and individual satisfaction; but that you are willing to sustain the perfect pattern and design which an Intelligence greater than your own has created, so that through you the entire race may be benefitted.

May I say here that, in the creation of this planet Earth, after We had responded to the call of Hercules and WILLED to create; after We had looked into the world of the Silent Watcher and PERCEIVED what Beloved Helios and Vesta wished Us to do; after Our hearts were filled with LOVE for this opportunity to give greater service, We were absolutely selfless in Our desire to create the Earth exactly as Helios and Vesta had designed It and We stayed with that perfect pattern until it was brought forth in great beauty, symmetry and perfection of every kind. Remember, as Elohim (Divine Builders of Creation in this entire Galaxy!) We were not only working with the planet Earth at that time but also in other Galaxies; for We are connected with many

Stars and other Systems. Having within Our consciousnesses many other designs of equal beauty and perfection, We just had to clear Our minds of all other ideas than those provided Us for this sweet Earth. *None of Us presumed · to suggest the changing of the form of even a blade of grass!* We voluntarily made Our consciousnesses like panes of clear glass, as it were, so that the light pattern designed by Those Great Ones (Helios and Vesta) could shine through Our consciousness and manifest. We would not even have started this creation if We had not been willing to lovingly co-operate with Its Designers!

Fifth: The next activity is that of CONCENTRATION and CONSECRATION from the Beloved Vista—the quality and ability to stay with one project until it is completed. Here again we come to that which is a great test to the lifestream. The vital fires of joyous enthusiasm and zeal which are kindled within the earnest student when he first touches the Truth of this light, usually turn to ash within about six months.

However, CONCENTRATION upon the same plan, pattern or design until it is physically manifest, is essential to the producing of *instantaneous* Precipitation. I have watched the activities of the inner bodies of the students many times—particularly during this series of addresses given by the Elohim. Every time one of Us has spoken on His particular activity, nearly everyone present determines within himself to draw forth and develop that quality of Mastery! You see, this is quite natural because, while you are in the radiation of Our consciousness and *feeling* of that Mastery, *it seems so very easy of accomplishment to you* and so much worth while. Now, these addresses have been given over a period of several months and, during that time, I can count on the fingers of one hand those who have stayed with the same pattern which they determined to develop some weeks ago.

If you are designing a car, a home, a garment to wear or whatever you may choose to precipitate, stay with one design until you have followed through the necessary "Seven Steps to Precipitation" which are scientifically required to manifest what you desire, visible and tangible in your outer use. It is not so important just *what you choose to precipitate,* but *it is important that you clearly understand the Science of Precipitation.* When you do and you are successfully able to use that Science *consciously* and at will, then, as your Master Saint Germain has previously said: "the things of this world will seem as rubbish to you." However, that which We are endeavoring to make you *feel,* is the joy which you can have in your conscious use of the power which is within you to produce that very manifestation. When you have done it once, the use of that power is yours for all Eternity and the faith, confidence and happiness that wells up in your heart will make you know and feel your Mastery.

Sixth: (Important: In the Science of conscious Precipitation, the Seventh Ray of RHYTHM of INVOCATION *precedes* the activity of sealing your manifestation in the substance and radiation of GOD-PEACE, which is normally the activity of the Sixth Ray.)

Seventh: After you have finished with the Fifth Ray of CONCENTRATION and have stayed with one pattern long enough, you come into the activity of Arcturus—RHYTHM OF INVOCA-TION. Here again, if you are serving the Master, it is of little effect if you serve Him in a great rush of energy one day and then do not show up again for a month! All the activities of Nature are in perfect RHYTHM. Watch your Seasons, sun-rises and sunsets, the ebb and flow of the tides and the regular beat of your own heart. Here you can see something of the necessity for RHYTHM. No matter what you are creating, the RHYTHM of feeding that pattern with your life by your thought, feeling and spoken decree at the same time each day—morning, noon and night (or what-ever time you decide to give to it) —is absolutely essential to your success in such endeavor.

In this regard, may I just give this warning, dear hearts? If you do not give your pattern of precipitation RHYTHM, you will bring forth a form without symmetry—*if you bring forth any-thing at all!* Some of the less beautiful of your architectural productions and—forgive Me for men-tioning this—but some of the imperfections of

your flesh forms are due to the unpleasant effects
of broken RHYTHM. Now, you who are conscious students "shy away" from broken rhythm
in the world of music and yet, in your own worlds,
that broken RHYTHM of thought, feeling, spoken
word and deed result so often in ill health, lack
of finances, lack of peace and many other limitations. In past Golden Ages of Perfection which
have been upon this dear Earth, *all the people*
walked with a rhythmic step and breathed the
slow rhythmic breath, because the perfect
RHYTHM of the Three-fold Flame within their
hearts was allowed to govern their life-energies
as they flowed into and through their four lower
bodies. As the Beloved Arcturus has said to you—
you could not long remain angry or resent-
ful if you were to govern the RHYTHM of the
life flowing through your bodies, by maintaining
the rhythmic breath at all times. Those of you
who have studied the art of rhythmic breathing
know something about this of which I speak.

In the case of drawing forth into visibility to
the physical sight of all, these Flames of the Sacred
Fire from the so-called "invisible" (which We
do wish to do in some of these Sanctuaries of the
New Activity—particularly where there is an already gathered focus and momentum of tremendous proportions in the ethers above a
given locality where, in the past, there have been
Atlantean Temples of some specialized God-
quality) —such Flames can never come forth from

the invisible to the visible until you have a constant and rhythmic attendance upon the focus of such Flames. This constancy of service *must be established far beyond the slightest possibility of breaking such* RHYTHM *of attendance by the "pull" of any outside interest!*

Now, right here—as I look into your minds and worlds while I am speaking to you—may I suggest that the smaller the thing you choose to bring forth as your *first* precipitation, the less of your vital energies it will take. Do not start with something the size of a large building, for instance. Begin with something that your reason will not confute in the wee hours of the morning when you are alone with your own thoughts and out of the greater radiation of the class; when you take time out during the day for your rhythmic attendance upon your project or during the day when you are engaged in the business of making a living and the pressures of the outer world are upon you. You can prove My words true in all of this —*if you will.*

Sixth: Then, O beloved ones, My heart pleads with you to *prayerfully consider* this final "step"— probably because it is My Own activity. After you have drawn forth your magnificent precipitation, seal it in My Flame of PEACE. Please do not allow any inharmony of any kind from yourself or others to destroy it. Just as you would place a cellophane cover over something precious which you wished to preserve, seal your precipitated form

in the Golden Flame of the Elohim of PEACE
and hold it inviolate against the disintegrating
forces of human thought and feeling. Perhaps the
greatest disintegrating force of such human
thought and feeling is the jealousy and doubt
of others.

Here let Me warn you—those of you who wish
to practice the Power of Precipitation—that it is
most important for you to *remain absolutely silent
concerning what you are about!* Seal your lips
against giving even an intimation through the
spoken word as to what you are doing for, believe
Me, you have no idea of the violence of feeling
which will be driven at you from those who are
covetous of your light's greater development.
Their own feelings of insecurity would make
them act thus toward you.

When the original creation of this planet was
finally manifest; when the activities of the
RHYTHM of Arcturus had drawn the final invocation of energy necessary for the completion
of this planet; when the Seven-fold Flame of the
Elohim had done Its perfect work; when the planet
Earth began to revolve upon Its axis and began
to release into the atmosphere Its melodious keynote to enhance the Music of the Spheres,—it was
a beautiful sight and sound indeed! At that time,
the PEACE which surpasses the understanding
of the human mind abided in the atmosphere of
the planet. However, when those "laggard" souls
came here from the other Systems and brought

disintegration through the feelings of rebellion, pride, hate, doubt and fear,—just like the well-known activity of the "Trojan horse"—from within out—the great perfection which had been established for so long began to recede here.

Precipitation—A Naturally Used Power on Lemuria and Atlantis

In your outer consciousness you do not remember, but We remember well the glorious perfection which was once upon this Earth when the Archangel Michael first reigned here. During the days of the perfection of light's dominion on Lemuria, when every man, woman and child wielded the powers of Precipitation and Etherialization just as easily as you draw breath today, at each meal time the patriarch of every household sat with his family around him and their table was spread with every good and perfect thing in the way of food and drink for the sustaining of the health and perfection of their bodies, minds and worlds. When the meal was finished, the mistress of the house, by the use of the power of Etherialization, removed the remains of the meal and the vessels used for its serving, without the raising of a hand. At that time, also, the ladies of the household created garments of beauty and perfection for the entire family by the use of their own thought and feeling centers and exercised the power of Precipitation by following through Its Seven Steps.

At this time, of course, all the energies of the soul-life of the people were devoted to the worship of God and expanding the borders of His Kingdom. On Atlantis, to a more limited degree, that same perfection existed in the Temples of Precipitation. In many of the more highly developed civilizations of the past, this activity of *conscious, instantaneous* Precipitation was the daily way of life of the people but why did this perfection not endure? WHY? *Because they lost the power of* SUSTAINED PEACE!

Now, again, you who have given your interest and your life to the activities of the Seventh Ray represented by Our Beloved Saint Germain, are slowly but surely emerging from the mire of human creation and limitation. We are endeavoring to build again a great foundation for this World Movement; trying to make of each of you a mighty pillar of Violet Fire. But, I can tell you here and now that, unless you HOLD UNINTERRUPTED PEACE as separate individuals and collective units —no matter how perfectly you build (nor with what perfect substance), you would have but ash in the end as long as there was still within the consciousness of any worker the disintegrating radiations of the "seven mortal sins" and all their ramifications.

To you who are Sanctuary and Group Directors, as well, of course, as to any sincere student who will ask Me for it, I shall give you *My* feeling of PEACE but *be sure you guard that* PEACE in your own individual feelings, in your homes and in all your activities—if you want sustained perfection.

Every Group Member Important!

Now let us consider for a moment the radiation which goes forth from the energies released by those who attend the group meetings. Let Me tell you that the type of radiation and outpouring of light's blessings drawn forth from Our Realm by your calls (which radiation sometimes completely envelops the Earth) may be determined by the very least of you. You know, self-depreciation is a very subtle and dangerous feeling and it is one of the tools used by the forces of evil to keep people from feeling that each one present becomes a part of the Cosmic magnet to draw the perfection from Our Realms into yours. Some certain God-quality or some Ascended Master's Presence might be drawn into this Octave through the group work in answer to a heart-call from one lifestream in the group—someone who seems quite insignificant to the outer senses but who has a certain harmonious attunement and spiritual power.

Then, too, let us not allow ourselves to be depressed in any way in these meetings but let us hold to a feeling of joyous enthusiasm, if we are in earnest about desiring to "widen the borders of the Kingdom". The sphere of influence of the class is determined by the quality of the en-

ergy in the worlds of every one present. Whenever possible, We come into an already builded
and qualified "forcefield" and that "forcefield" is
expanded by invocations, decrees, songs and enthusiastic feelings of every blessed member of that
audience. This activity can be likened unto a
wheel which is lying on its side; the hub is in
the center, of course, and the spokes go from it
in every direction to its rim (periphery). The size
of this wheel of radiation is increased by the release of the combined energies from each one
present. The larger the hub of the wheel (number
present in the group), the greater the energy released to expand the radiations of the class farther
and farther afield. Your own personal light might
be the very last bit of radiation needed to make
the activity world-engulfing and, without that
light, such radiation might fall short of that world-
enfolding service.

I cannot speak of this too emphatically! Each
student in the group represents a radiating center of some God-quality and is drawn into the
group by the Powers of Light already accumulated
in his or her own Causal Body all through the
centuries. Every lifestream present contributes to
the sphere of influence of that group, which influence can become world-engulfing. If the group
is small in numbers and the enthusiasm rather
"lukewarm", it can but render just a localized
service. In the case of this class here today, We
have been enabled to completely encircle the

planet Earth by the release of your energies. I am now speaking not only to you but through you to those whom you will contact in the future, for you are to be the teachers of this Law at a later time. You are the men and women who are going to have to answer many questions from the "lukewarm" and vaguely interested. The better your understanding of the truth and efficacy of this Law; the better your knowledge and application of It and just what takes place when It is invoked, the more answers you will have ready to give to your inquirers and the greater will be your service as arms of Ourselves in action.

Groups Form Magnetic Field

Your group activities form a magnetic field of energy which draws Intelligences and Beings from the Realms of Light above the human octave, Who have fully developed Their Own God-mastery and Who are willing and able to give Their full-gathered momentums of that perfection to you and to all who will ask for and accept it. Through the release of the energy in definite visualization, as well as through the spoken word released in invocations, decrees and songs, there is formed this magnetic field of energy ("forcefield") just referred to, which connects with the energies of the Higher Octaves, into which those energies are directed. This makes a sort of "funnel", cutting right through the shadowed substance of the Astral or

Psychic Realm,—"funnel" of light into the Realm of Perfection. What then flows down through that "funnel"? Electronic fire from Our Octave! That "fire" is the purity and power of the feelings of masterful perfection from the Ascended Beings. At your call, one or more of the Great Ones in Our Realm Whose attention you have drawn by that call, directs His consciously qualified light-substance to you here.

For instance, when you magnetize the Beloved Archangel Michael, just what happens? First you draw His attention and consicousness to you by your call to Him, with your thought and feeling thus fixed upon Him. The moment your attention goes to any Perfected Being, that moment His "virtue" automatically flows out from Him (or Her) to you. That energy is sent to you in the form of a Ray of light, made up of what we shall call for simplicity and clarification—"electrons". This sending forth of the Ray by the Ascended Master is a *descending activity*. Then, when that Ray reaches the world of the one who has called for assistance, what happens? That same Ray, qualified with the blessing necessary to answer the call for help from the supplicant, immediately begins its *ascent* back to its Sender as *living Flame*. The very nature of the Flame is always to rise and so, this Ray of perfected light energy passes as Flame up through the four lower bodies of the supplicant (physical, etheric, mental and emotional), as well as through the atmosphere around that one.

This activity of the rising Flame then completes the Law of the Circle—the Ray which the Master sent forth returning eventually to Him with the added blessing of the service rendered to the supplicant. Such returning Flame then adds to the glory of that Master's Causal Body. Whatever purification and blessing has taken place in the world of the unascended one is a *permanent gift* from the Master to that one. *However, through the exercise of his own free-will, that unascended one, by allowing momentums of certain destructively qualified energy from the past to act through habits of thought, feeling, spoken word and deed, may re-create all over again the same distresses from which he has been set free!*

In the case of the Beloved Michael, He directs His attention to the supplicant through that "funnel" of which We spoke before and, because all Perfected Beings desire only to expand God's goodness, Lord Michael desires only to pour the radiation and feeling of His Mastery of energy to you to help you. This is His gift of faith, confidence, enthusiasm and positively qualified energy into and through your world, the worlds of all you contact and into the general atmosphere of Earth. If you are holding your world in a state of sustained harmony and PEACE at all times, you then become a living "conductor" of the fire of God-perfection into this physical appearance world and this "fire" purifies and raises in consciousness everyone and everything it touches. Thus can you make of yourselves a constantly radiating center of light's perfection which can go to the very ends of the Earth, if necessary.

Explanation of "Chakric" Centers

Now, part of My assignment which was given to Me to include in this morning's service is a brief explanation of the "chakric" centers in your bodies. You see, whatever takes place here in this "forcefield"—the heart-center of Our New Activity —affects every individual belonging to this Movement. When We offer one of these Quarterly Classes, some are fortunate enough to feel it a real necessity to come into Our direct Presence to receive the gifts We have to give. Although some seem to feel it quite unnecessary to come, bringing their physical bodies here and so receive the blessings of such classes direct from Us, they are still the beneficiaries of them to a certain extent, since the radiation blazes forth at such times from this "forcefield" to all who are interested in Us. This morning, every gentle reader of our literature (especially "The Bridge" and "The Bulletin") on every Continent of the planet, is having assistance from Us today.

When We endeavor so to draw you together in one place this way, it is that We may give to your bodies, minds and feeling worlds, a definite service.

For a moment, let us consider the "chakric" centers in your etheric body, corresponding to the ganglionic nerve centers in your flesh. You know, the word "chakra" is an Oriental word meaning "wheel."

As you have been told, the Seven Rays of the Seven Mighty Elohim are anchored in the fore-head of every physical form and, through the ex-pansion of these, We are able to reach into your worlds to help you, if you will allow Us so to do. Of course, We never intrude in any way, for your God-given gift and prerogative of the use of your own free-will is always paramount! You see, from the beginning, it was intended that the Elohim, Archangels, Chohans of the Rays and Angelic Host were to be in *constant daily association* with mankind, as They are on Venus and other planets; *and have been,* all through the ages. However, the "veil of maya" (effluvia of discord) gradually became so very thick around the planet Earth and the actual bodies of the people, that We could not get through to their consciousness at all. I think there has never been a recorded time on this planet when the Elohim and Archangels have spoken to the people of Earth in consecutive order as has been done here recently. I believe the Chohans have.

In the etheric body are seven centers which are called, in Oriental terminology, the "chakras". These *should* carry the positive, clear, constructive colors representing the colors of the Seven Rays of the Chohans, the Archangels and Ourselves. These "centers" were meant to be convex in shape and radiating foci of the qualities of perfection of the Seven Rays. Instead, because of centuries lived in discordant vibrations, these have become concave,—declivities in the etheric body. Therefore, instead of being radiating centers of God-perfection, through long ages of human experience, these declivities have become filled with the destructive, humanly-qualified vibrations and have become the roots of the "seven mortal sins", with many ramifications. If you will call to Me to help you in such activity, I shall be glad to help you to root out the *causes and cores* of these destructive vibrations and, drawing these centers from a depressed form, make them convex in shape again. When this condition has been so corrected, I can then re-charge these centers with the positive radiations *which they should have.* Then, instead of being so negative and so easily accessible to the particular distresses which disturb you individually, you can then be a positive radiating center for the qualities of the Elohim, the Archangels and the Chohans of the Rays, if you so choose. No one needs to accept this assistance unless he desires to have it!

Previously, We have not discussed these "centers" with you because, under the Law of the New Day and the Ascended Master Saint Germain's Activity, the attention of the students is to be focused only upon the three upper centers of the body. But, when the call went up from you this morning for the removal from yourselves, all under this radiation and all mankind, of the causes and cores of the "seven mortal sins", through the intercession to the Great Karmic Board of Beloved Kwan Yin (Goddess of Mercy), We have permission to speak briefly on these "chakras" today.

Each "chakra" should be like a wheel moving rapidly in a clock-wise rotation and the more rapid the vibratory action of these "chakric" centers in your four lower vehicles, the more non-recordant they will be to discord. This is one of the services rendered by your rapidly spoken decrees and quick tempo of your music. Please remember, though, that this is not to be confused with the idea of "hurry". All along the way, it requires the use of the student's discrimination— it is really the way of "the razor's edge". "Hurry", in itself, is destructive and is to be avoided at all costs by the sincere student. However, a rapid, positive vibration quickens the energies of the four lower bodies and makes one repellant to feelings of depression, doubt, fear, lethargy and all of the various sins of the human; except, perhaps, the qualities of pride and rebellion, which move at a very quick rate and are more subtle than some of the others. These negative vibrations may get into the student's world either from within his own accumulations of discord which are recorded in his own etheric body and are sometimes brought to the surface by the outer consciousness through recalled memory; or they may be floating in the atmosphere in which he moves; or they may be consciously directed at him and his world by others who have been caught in destructive activities.

These "chakras" in the etheric body are supposed to be like suns of their particular color— magnetic centers for the drawing into the world of the individual the radiations of the perfection of the qualities which they represent from the Elohim, Archangels and Chohans of the Seven Rays. In the Jewish religion and in other religions where they use the Seven Jewels of Light on the Altar, these Jewels are representative, not only of the Seven Rays, but also of these centers within the etheric body and, through the etheric body, to the physical body.

The lowest "chakra" which is at the base of the spine is the focus of lust and passion in the spiritually unawakened. This is its *negative* aspect. In the "awakened", it is the *positive* focus of Purity. The Elohim in charge of that "chakra" is the Elohim of Purity; the Archangel Who should pour His radiation of the Resurrection Flame through it is Gabriel and the Ascended Master is Serapis Bey (Who, when allowed to blaze the purity of His Ascension Flame through this "chakra", assists the individual to the victory of the Ascension). *Please do not put undue attention upon this.*

The central "chakra", located at the spleen, is the focus of anger, malice, hatred and even mild dislike, in its *negative* aspect. Its *positive* activity is the power of Invocation. The Elohim in charge of this center is Arcturus; its Archangel is Zadkiel and its Ascended Master is Saint Germain.

The "chakra" at the solar plexus is the focus of greed, gluttony, covetousness and fear in its *negative* aspect. That is why you feel "struck" in the solar plexus when you are suddenly fearful. People are gluttonous and covetous because they are fearful that they either are not receiving or that they will not receive their just share of the good they should have. The *positive* quality of this "chakra" is PEACE and this focus is that over which I am in charge as the Elohim of PEACE. The Archangel Who radiates through this center is Uriel and the Ascended Master is Our Beloved Nada. This is one of the reasons why, early in your study of these Laws of Life, you were asked to visualize the luminous Presence of Jesus in dazzling white light surrounded by gold * on the forehead and over the solar plexus of yourself and others. When this "chakra" has been completely purified and you hold the solar plexus in a wholly controlled manner, feeling the radiation of Ascended Master PEACE from My Own humble Self, Uriel and Nada, then you will have complete protection against both fear and the

---

* For further explanation please see "The Bridge to Freedom," Vol. 6, No. 1: P. 22. As before mentioned, our Beloved Lady Master Nada recently has been accepted by the Cosmic Law as the Chohan of the Sixth Ray, replacing the Beloved Jesus in this office, as He and blessed Kuthumi jointly have been accepted as World Teacher.

destructive desires of others of mankind; as well
as complete protection from the "grasping" nature
of your own physical appetites.

The "chakra" at the heart, in the *negative*
aspect, represents lethargy, sloth and laziness.
If your *heart* is not in a thing, you do not give it
much of your life. The *positive* radiation of this
center, of course, is that of pure, selfless, Divine
Love. Its Elohim is the Beloved Orion; the Archangel is Chamuel and the Chohan is the Ascended
Master Paul, the Venetian, Who represents toler-
ance and "His brother's keeper".

The "chakra" at the throat is the power center
of the body where, in its *negative* aspect, rests
envy and the desire for personal power. Its *positive* activity is the power to create perfection by the
doing of God's Will and, the Elohim in charge here
is Hercules; the Archangel is Lord Michael and the
Chohan is Beloved El Morya.

The "chakra" in the forehead is the focus of
the power of reason and its *negative* aspects manifest as pride and intellectual arrogance. It is the
place where doubt is allowed to enter the mind.
Its *positive* aspect is visualized in early mythology
as the "all-seeing-eye" of God and the power of
Concentration. The Elohim Whose name is Vista
(Whom you have known through the years as
"Cylopea") is the One in charge of this center.
The Archangel in charge of this "chakra" is Beloved Raphael Who is the Archangel of Concentration and Consecration. No lifestream will con-

secrate himself to anything until both his mind and heart are convinced of the efficacy of the service he can render through such endeavors. The Ascended Master Hilarion represents that focus also. That is why, as Saint Paul (formerly Saul of Tarsus), He had the tremendous mental development of the Fifth Ray (the Ray of which He is today in charge).

Thank God that the "crown-center" of the body (at the very top of the head) has not been touched destructively and there is no negative vibration there. In most people, this center is completely undeveloped but, in the earnest student, when the attention is rhythmically turned to his own Beloved "I Am" Presence anchored within his own heart, this center begins to throb and eventually forms an aureole or halo of light about the head. Finally, it comes to a point where, with the inner sight at first, you can see a blazing halo of living light around the head of the sincere student. This is the "chakra" presided over by Beloved Cassiopea, the Elohim of Illumination; its Archangel is Beloved Jophiel and the Ascended Master is our dear Kuthumi. Of course, His Ray is that of Illumination and all who start upon the Spiritual Path first come under the direction and instruction of Beloved Kuthumi.

Now, We have given you a great deal this morning— yet *you must have this information and knowledge if you are to move forward into greater light! In the Name of God—*dear people—*after*

you have received this instruction—PLEASE USE
IT! You are going to be Doctors of Spiritual
Philosophy and you should have everything essential for such service right at your "finger-tips", if
you are to be of help to your "patients". You
should be thoroughly familiar with the names and
activities of all the Elohim and Their Divine
Complements; the Archangels and Their Archaii
(feminine counterparts of the Archangels); the
Chohans (Lords) of the Seven Rays (Their activities also representing the positive functions of the
ganglionic centers—"chakras" just referred to);
the use of the various activities of the Sacred Fire;
the powers of magnetization and radiation and—
most important of all—*the capacity to do it yourself!* . . . .

Evolution of the Elohim of Peace

Some of you already know that the evolution of
the Elohim is through the Elemental Kingdom
(El-e-mental meaning "mind of God"). Each of
Us started out as small Elemental beings, belonging to different Systems, different Galaxies, at
different times. I was one among those Elementals
Who followed the exact order of creation. You
have seen Universal Elemental Light filling the
atmosphere; those tiny electrons seem to be going
nowhere—just flitting hither and yon in the sun-
shine. You see, when one is first God-created,
there is complete freedom to just enjoy one's self.

That is where some folks get the idea of Heaven as being a place of eternal enjoyment, rest and the general "do-as-you-please" attitude. *They remember backward*—for this is not looking forward—and I warn you ahead of time—*the future is not going to be like that!* Those were your "pre-Eden days"!

Long, long ago, I was one of these tiny Elementals, flitting hither and yon in My Universe; whenever I felt like it, attaching Myself to some Light Ray projected by some Being of Whom I was scarcely cognizant. At times, I rode upon a great beam of that light which was destined to become part of a Star or some other lovely God-creation. I had no responsibilities and no obligations.

This same freedom is given to all of God's creations—for instance, your "I Am" Presence, when first created, was permitted to go through each of the Seven Spheres of activity around Its God-head (Its Source) ; find that Sphere in which It was most interested; stay in any Temple as long as It liked; at the feet of any Master for any length of time It desired. The Angels have like freedom. When first created, They disport Themselves in the glory and light of the body of God and, eventually, become a part of the Virtues of Faith, Hope, Charity or any God-virtue They please. These Angels live in the Temples of Their choice—They absorb and *just are!*

Then, suddenly, one day there came a feeling

within Me that I wanted to be a *conscious* part of creation. When this takes place within anyone, it means that the activity of the First Ray is born within them—the WILL TO DO. So it was with Me.

Then I sought out someone whom I knew could tell Me just what to do and, when I had found such an one, I was told that, if I cared to go to a certain Nature Temple, I could learn how to build form—perhaps a flower. To do this, together with others of like intent, I had to learn to hold the thought-form shown to Us on the Altar by the presiding Deva, Our Instructor. After enrolling Myself as a student in this Nature Temple, My first assignment was to build a five-petalled, yellow flower *and I shall never forget it!* O, there must have been a couple of hundred of Us in the class— all quite as irresponsible as Myself. We could hear beautiful music outside the Temple; the air was so lovely and fresh; beautiful Beings of Light were passing through the atmosphere outside the windows,—and the holding of the pattern of that flower got *so monotonous,* I can tell you! However, the Deva just stood there on the Altar and from Himself He externalized the pattern of this flower which We were to learn to create. He tried to catch Our thoughts and focus them upon that flower. But, I soon found that just the WILL TO DO was not enough—there must follow the other six "steps" of creation to perfect the activity.

Then, suddenly, PERCEPTION came into My

mind and I thought—"Yes, *this is* a part of creation" and I PERCEIVED, at least, what the Deva
wanted Me to try to do. Up until that time, I just
enjoyed the fragrance, the color and the symmetry
of form of that flower. I did not feel that I wanted
to do anything more than that about it. As that
feeling of PERCEPTION took possession within
Me, I consciously tried. O, but that first form
which I attempted to create was certainly a distorted one—it was sort of square; it did not have
enough petals; nor did it have the right fragrance.
Besides, just as soon as I took My attention away
from it—the form was gone! Now, some in the class
were still not very concentrated in their attention
and were still "flitting around". However, those
of Us Who really meant business finally moved
up to the front of the room, nearer the Altar.

Well, as We continued to absorb the instruction
and tried again and again, finally, one day, the
little yellow flower appeared in My hands and I
was so happy! This time I had the right number
of petals, the right color and the right fragrance
for My flower but—My goodness! just as I was
about to present it to the Deva, one of the Archangels went by the window and My attention
being drawn by His magnificent light, it left the
flower for an instant. When I looked back at My
hand—the flower was gone! Just a lack of Concentration, you see!

Now these Devas do not speak at all. They give
all Their instruction through radiation and Our

Teacher Deva suggested to Us that if We wanted to create these flowers *consciously*, We could add beauty and perfection to a Springtime on some lovely planet which the Elohim in charge of that planet were to beautify for the blessing of an evolution of living souls. As I thought of this, LOVE for My endeavor was born within Me —I felt that I wanted to make that little flower perfect enough, fragrant enough, beautiful enough and make it last long enough to really bless some part of life. That was the third aspect of Divinity —LOVE—you see! Then I forgot *Myself* and the distraction of Those who were going by outside; then I really wanted to create that flower and I stayed with it!

What happened then? I received an assignment. The Devas do not assign one to the task of even becoming an apple-blossom until They know you will stay with that task long enough to complete it. In My new assignment, I think there were about seven hundred of Us directed to adorn one big tree. Incidentally, the yellow flower I was to create does not grow on your Earth— nor does such a tree. Perhaps, one day it shall.

Here came another lesson which I did not learn at once. Our Teacher reminded Us that when We went to that planet with the Great Deva of the tree to be formed, We would see all different kinds ot trees. He warned Us to watch and see that Our individual flower to be created did not become just like that which We saw on some other shrub

or tree. I forgot His admonition and Mine did!
I saw pink flowers, blue ones and white ones and,
by the time I was through looking at them all,
I had nothing definite of My Own in mind—
and therefore no manifestation.

Then I learned the fourth lesson—the PURITY
of holding to the Divine pattern which had been
given Me in the beginning. When We finally went
back to Our Nature Temple "schoolroom", none of
Us Who had "lost out" was at all proud of His accomplishments. You see, Those in charge always
prepare more Elementals than They know will be
needed for a certain creation and, therefore, the
creation was completed by those who could do
the work. I did not volunteer so quickly for the
next experience, I can tell you! However, within
Myself, I determined that I would hold the pattern
of that yellow flower until I had brought it forth
in perfection.

Finally, I did not even have to volunteer. My
Teacher Deva, in mercy, said to Me, one day:
"All right—you may go and try again". This
time I closed My eyes, My mind and My attention to everything but to the *becoming* of that yellow flower. Yet, there remained even more for Me
to remember—CONSTANCY—for I allowed My
petals to fall before the Springtime was over! I
had to learn the fifth activity of CONSTANCY
and CONCENTRATION until the Deva called
Me home. Because of My lack of CONSTANCY,
after the premature falling of My petals, *I was*

home a whole month before the others! I must tell
you that I did not go into the Temple for quite
a while—I walked up and down outside but I did
not go in! At last, I had to go in—you know that!
Wherever you are and whatever you volunteer to
do. you must finish it one day. It is the same
thing with humanity—they may "play around"
as long as they wish and waste their time but, one
day they must finish their course (fulfill their
Divine Plan). Sooner or later, perhaps with your
feathers trailing, you will go back to the fulfilling
of your original Divine Plan.

When We gathered again before the Deva in
the Nature Temple, I was seated far back in the
last row. I was small of stature and I thought
I would not be too easily seen there. Thinking
to Myself, I said: "I shall never go out again.
I'll just stay right here". However, next We were
taught the lesson of RHYTHM.

Here I learned that I had to hold the purity
of form and that I had to stay at My post until
I was released by the Being Who had sent Me
forth. That was CONSTANCY. Then, amazingly,
I learned that I had to go *every* Spring! My
goodness! I thought going once was a major
achievement, but I learned the lesson of RHYTHM
—yellow flower—yellow flower—yellow flower—
over and over again, *each and every Spring.* I
shall not atempt to tell you how many Springtimes
I became a yellow flower. Doing it once was a
novelty; even a dozen times was fun; but *every*

Spring seemed to Me like a long, steady, relent-
less "grind"! Obedience! Obedience! Obedience!
to the end!

The last step I had to learn in this process of
creation was to HOLD THE PEACE. The last
time that Deva told Me that I was going to be a
yellow flower again—*I nearly lost the whole
course!!!* You see, in the meantime, others of My
friends had become beautiful trees, shrubs and
other lovely creations but *I was still* a little, tiny
yellow flower. So, you see, I had to learn to HOLD
THE PEACE—PEACE which I became Myself
—mind you —in a far-distant future scheme!
So, if you are one of those "little yellow flowers",
learn to HOLD YOUR PEACE! Perhaps, one
day, you will be a Sun to a System! Who knows
what anyone's use of free-will may do?

At last, on this final trip, I just *let go!* I really
did! I thought: "If God wills it, I shall be this
blossom for eternity!" That was My last trip!
That absolute surrender gave Me My release
and, that time, when I returned to My Deva in
the Nature Temple, He crowned My service of
the ages—AGES I SAID!—with Victory! Then
I was graduated into the Devic Kingdom.

For a long, long time, I served and worked with
increasing efficiency until I finally took the initia-
tion of the Elohim. Later, when given opportunity
by the call from Beloved Helios and Vesta for
Those Who would volunteer to build for Them
this dear planet Earth, I voluntarily joined the

other six Elohim to render that service. We served together in association, both for the joy of comradeship and the joy of creation.

Now, proceeding through these "Seven Steps" of activity is the way by which the Elohim expand Their consciousness from an Elemental being to a great Builder of Form; it is the way by which the tiny Cherubim become great Devas of light and, passing through those "steps" also, the spiritually unawakened soul eventually awakens and becomes the great Ascended Being of Love, Light and Perfection. There is no escape from the following of those "Seven Steps" anywhere. Some natures are such that they accept and follow those "steps" quickly and some take a longer time to accomplish. Believe Me, I know! I think I was the slowest pupil of all the grouping of Elementals with Whom I started out but, one thing I learned (if nothing else) was to HOLD MY PEACE *and abide in the wisdom of the Law!*

For the kindness and courtesy of your attention and for your love, I thank you! Will you remember always, please, that PEACE IS A POSITIVE POWER! I—Who have passed the way of evolution before you—I am yours to command! I leave with you My blessings. May all your precipitations be perfect; your "flowers" beautiful and all your God-endeavors successful in His Name! Thank you and Good morning!

EXPLANATORY

As our Gentle Reader will see from the dates on
the preceding addresses personally given by The
Seven Mighty Elohim of Creation, these discourses came forth here in the Philadelphia Sanctuary of the New Activity of our Beloved Ascended
Master Saint Germain and Beloved El Morya,
over a period of some four months—from Septem-
ber 5th, 1954 to January 2nd, 1955. Since that
time, a great deal of purification has gone on
within the Earth, on Its surface and in Its atmosphere. Particularly have there been tremendous
changes through purification in the so-called
"inner realms" around the Earth. Mark you!
These are not the Realms of Light of which we
are speaking now—but the spheres of discordant
thought and feeling, spoken word and deed which
are "invisible" to the physical sight of most of
Earth's people. This of which we speak is the
accumulation of the ages of such discordantly
qualified life released from Earth's people and is
that which has brought about so much distress
and destruction here. This destructive creation
around the Earth (which the Great Ones often
speak of as "human effluvia") exists in different
strata of vibration and extends out around the
Earth to at least the 10,000 foot altitude.

The "Compound"

One of the most distressing of the foci of destruction within Earth's atmosphere was that which the Ascended Masters have called the "Compound". Here had been magnetically drawn together certain unfortunate individuals who had allowed the energies of their lifestreams to become very destructive for a long, long period of time and, after passing from the body at the close of each embodiment, their various appetites and habits were of such a nature that they could not rise out of the atmosphere of the planet where they had not only developed those destructive activities within and around themselves, but had imposed them upon other lifestreams as well. "Like attracts like" and the very destructively qualified energy they had released on Earth, being connected, of course, with their own individual worlds, then bound them to the very planet they had helped to despoil.

As our blessed Earth is the only planet in all creation where there is discord of any kind and where such discord has been allowed to accumulate and condense as it has here, there was no other place to which these unfortunate individuals could go—even between embodiments—for instruction, purification and preparation for a better life next time. Why? Because of each individual's use of his God-given prerogative of free-will. Although many invitations to do so were offered to these lifestreams by the Messengers of the Great Karmic

Board Who were sent to them from time to time, these individuals steadfastly refused to leave the Earth and Its environs because, living in their own discordant rates of vibration, they were more comfortable in the shadows of the Astral or Psychic plane. Light is very discomfiting and very uncomfortable to those whose motives, desires and activities are not of God. You know that this is so with even bright, physical light—destructively qualified consciousnesses prefer darkness in which to do their nefarious deeds. How much more, then, would their feelings be disturbed by the intense power of the purity of the light which fills interstellar space, outside of the periphery of the Earth's atmosphere?

Incidentally, the Great Ones have told us that there has been established a "shut-off", so to speak, around the periphery of Earth's atmopshere which prevents the destructive vibrations of our planet from expanding into the perfect and harmonious interstellar realms. It is because of this accumulation of human discord which shuts in the light of our planet and Her people which has made our Earth known for so long as "The Dark Star". She has emitted no light of Her Own nor from the evolutions belonging to Her, for aeons of time!

Today, thank God! all this is being changed and our sweet Earth (once such a dazzling Jewel of beauty and perfection in the Crown of God's great Universe) is now being purified by the tremendous assistance being given, not only by Her Own

Creators (Beloved Helios and Vesta—God and Goddess of our physical Sun and God-parents of our planet; the Seven Mighty Elohim; Directors of the Forces of the Elements, etc.) but by transcendent Beings from other Galaxies and other Spheres of the Godhead. This could not be done for the planet until there was certain co-operation offered by some group of unascended humanity itself living upon this planet; those with whom our Beloved Saint Germain and others of the Ascended Host have worked so diligently for so long to spiritually awaken to the Truth concerning life upon this planet and all life everywhere. Thus have They stirred up within these lifestreams an enthusiastic desire to free—not only themselves and all they love—but, serving impersonally, free their fellowman and the entire planet as well. This has been done in part, at least, by instructing them in the use of the Violet Fire and other purifying actions of the Sacred Fire; showing them how, by the use of these purifying Flames (which would go into action immediately at their sincere call) they could raise the entire planet and all Her evolutions very quickly into the glorious light and perfection which the Earth was in the beginning. At the same time, the lifestreams so serving would be raising themselves and all they love out of the darkness of human limitations and distress into the complete purification of their own four lower bodies and then into the complete victory of the Ascension—the final goal of everyone's earthly pil-

grimage. To this end do those of us who are interested in such a project "keep on keeping on"
until the full perfection we desire is attained.

The "Compound" mentioned herein had been
existent for millions of years and, as Beloved Saint
Germain expressed it recently, it was like a great
"cancer" on the body of the Earth! Such a place
no longer exists anywhere in the Universe now.
All who had been within it have willingly come
forth from its unhappy darkness and are now consciously and co-operatively working to free themselves at Inner Levels of greater light where beautiful Temples of Instruction have been provided
for them by the Ascended Ones. In these they learn
how to transmute into light their mistakes of the
past, how to balance their accounts with life and
make things right. The Great Ones have told us
that, this year, a few of these lifestreams who had
been in the "Compound" for some time, are now
ready for physical embodiment here again and
will soon come through the Gates of Birth—this
time much more illumined as to how to live life
successfully. So, in the mercy of the Great Law, are
they given opportunity to try again to fulfill their
Divine Plan—the reason for which they were created in the beginning.

The "Sleepers' Realm"

The "Sleepers' Realm" referred to is still in
existence because there is a great need for some

place of peace and rest for the inner bodies of lifestreams who have finished an embodiment of very
strenuous activity—particularly when they have
been engaged in helping to set life free here from
the chains of human limitations and the suffering
of dis-ease. However, individuals are no longer
allowed to stay in this Realm indefinitely—just
because of their unwillingness to face reality. All
of those who had been there have come forth now,
consciously and willingly standing before the
Karmic Board to receive their assignments to persons, places, conditions and things which will enable them to progress in the fulfillment of their
own Divine Plan. Today, those passing from the
body who require such rest are allowed to remain
there only three months at the longest. There is
much interesting and instructive information concerning these Realms in our book "Memoirs of
Beloved Mary, Mother of Jesus".

Concerning the Astral or Psychic Plane around
the Earth, no longer are those who have been
"Earth-bound" allowed to remain in Earth's
atmosphere after so-called "death". These were
known as "discarnates" and their presence in
Earth's atmosphere was not only distressing to
others in their own Realm, but to those embodied
here as well. *Now*, as soon as one passes from the
body, he is taken to certain Temples of Light in
the Higher Realms where he is given assistance
toward a better embodiment next time. There
are no more *dis-embodied lifestreams* living in the

atmosphere of our planet now; those shadowed forms which still remain there are simply thought-forms of human creation which are sustained and expanded there by the constant feeding into them of the release of the mass of mankind's thoughtless and careless use of his own life in destructive thought, feeling, spoken word and deed. These *can be* dissolved and trans-muted into light by the use of the Sacred Fire of Purification at the call for Its service by those interested in giving such commands (de-crees) in the Name and Authority of their own individualized God-Presence, Whose Name is "I AM". (Old Testament, Exodus 3:14). When the cause and core of these creations of human discord have been completely removed from the Earth and the worlds of Her people, then will Her com-plete and eternal freedom come more quickly and She will be able to not only emit Her Own light but Her musical keynote as well; adding Her lovely harmonies to the Music of the Spheres which constantly plays and sings everywhere else in Creation.

"Karma"

The word "karma" as used in these addresses is, as you may know, a word used in the Orient to mean "come back". It refers to energy sent forth from some intelligence which, according to the Law of the Circle governing all creation, then re-turns to its sender after having reached the peri-

phery of the sphere of influence into which it was
sent forth. As it travels *from* its source and back
to it again, by the Law of Magnetic Attraction, it
draws to itself all of its kind which it contacts and
thus returns to its source *always with accumulated
energy.* Knowing this, one can easily see why
Beloved Jesus said: "It is more blessed to give
than to receive. . . ." for, when receiving, the
lifestream accepting that gift has the gift *alone;*
while the giver of that gift, having sent forth his
thought, feeling, spoken word and deed thus to
bless, later receives the return into his world of
the full-gathered momentum of all the accumulated good which his energy had contacted as it spun
around its circle of existence. So is every one the
greatest beneficiary of his own goodness expressed
(which returns to him amplified many fold) , and
he is also the greatest sufferer from the results of
his own mis-deeds which, likewise, return to their
source—and *always with accumulated energy!* Remember! This is one of the simplest and yet most
important of the Laws of Life and one which many
of mankind rather stubbornly refuse to cognize,
consider or obey—"whatsoever a man soweth—
that shall he also reap!" If we send out only good
to our fellowman and into the atmosphere of ourselves and the planet, nothing but good can return.
This "good" which we send out creates more light
in our individual worlds, as well as in and around
the planet itself for, "even the light of a penny
candle increases the light of the Sun". Also, that

light, in itself, will become an invincible protection to one as he gathers the momentum thereof. One's own "good" (God) is his most powerful protection *and the only protection he has which is absolutely invincible and eternal!*

The "Atomic Accelerator"

The "Atomic Accelerator" spoken of in the pages of this book is no figment of anyone's imagination! *At least one* of these magnificent chairs now abides within Beloved Saint Germain's Retreat, which is located somewhere in the western part of our United States. Beloved Saint Germain worked to perfect this chair during many of His embodiments before His Ascension took place. This "Atomic Accelerator" is made of precipitated golden light-substance and, when operated by an Ascended Master, can and does much more quickly raise the vibrations of the atomic structure of the physical and other three lower bodies of the one seated within that chair and being so assisted.

At the present time, such a service is very rarely permitted to be given to any unascended one by the Great Law and then, when it is, it could only be done by the granting of a special dispensation by the Great Karmic Board for the assisting of some lifestream who had volunteered to render an extraordinary service to life which had to be completely accomplished within a certain limited time.

You see, the present density of mankind's physical form is due to the slowing down of the vibrations of the electrons as they spin around their central core in the atom. When this vibratory action is not quickened sufficiently, the weight of the shadows which have been created by the individual's free-will use of discordant thought, feeling, spoken word and deed cannot be thrown off and simply lodges between the electrons in the atom. This shuts off the luminosity of the electrons and the light cannot shine through the flesh, as it did in the beginning of mankind's embodiments on this planet in the First Golden Age. In that day, all mankind's bodies were self-luminous and perfect and emitted their own light, quite naturally. No artificial lighting was required to be used at that time. Consciously accelerating the rates of vibration in His four lower bodies was that which enabled the Beloved Jesus to be transfigured in light as He was before Peter, James and John—the story with which we are all so familiar.

This "Atomic Accelerator" was used on Atlantis for the blessing of the people as a healing, purifying agent, although it was not in its fully perfected state then. Beloved Saint Germain has now perfected its activity since His Ascension and the Great Ones have promised us (as you will read herein) that such an assistance to mankind shall come forth for the blessing of the race when deemed advisable, in the wisdom of the Great Cosmic Law.

"Forcefields"

The subject of "forcefields" seems to be so little understood by so many and yet its explanation is simple in the extreme. A "forcefield" is just what its name implies—a "field of force"—constructively qualified energies which have been and are being released by those who are students of the Laws of Life under the direction, protection and radiation of the Ascended Host. There is much enlightening information concerning these in our "Transmission of the Flame" books, various issues of "The Bulletin" (back issues of which, in bound form, can now be obtained) and in various of the addresses by our Beloved Lord Maha Chohan which appear in back issues of "The Bridge to Freedom".

Etherealization

Etherealization is the science of returning instantly to the Universal again from whence it came, whatever form has been drawn forth by the use of the Powers of Precipitation—either because that form was distorted by some imperfect use of the Law or because that form had served the purpose for which it was created. Then the light essence of which it was composed is freed to return to the Sun for re-polarization.

The "Three-Fold-Flame of Eternal Truth"

This Focus of God-perfection anchored within the physical heart of every "personality", is composed of Three beautiful Plumes of brilliant, always active Flame—Blue (representing *energy*, which becomes *power* through use) ; Gold—the center Plume (representing Wisdom and Illumination) and the Pink Plume (representing Divine Love) on the right.

It is very beneficial for the student, sometime each day, to picture himself standing within a greatly expanded focus of such a Flame (having called forth Its expansion from the Three-fold Flame within his heart). The entire body should stand within the Gold Plume—visualizing It to have expanded to about twelve feet in height—our bodies in the center of It. That Flame then would, of course, extend out around the physical body for a foot or so. Next, see the lovely Blue Plume to the left of the body and the Pink Plume to the right.

In the average spiritually unawakened individual, this Flame is less than one-sixteenth of an inch in height! One can imagine the tremendous power within this Flame when so tiny a focus can keep a 200 (or more) pound body moving about all day, performing all its living functions, physically, mentally and emotionally! This tiny Flame has within Its heart an "airless cell" in which there abides a small focus of the "Holy Christ Self"—and this holds within the physical form an anchorage of the Flame of full Perfection from the heart of one's own individualized "I Am" Presence.

When the "outer self" has become sufficiently interested in knowing the Truth of his own being and begins to seek knowledge and wisdom (for Wisdom is the right use of knowledge) —then the Three-fold Flame within the heart begins to expand—slowly at first—but increases more rapidly as the "Holy Christ Self" is released from that "airless cell" at a certain point in the expansion of the Christ consciousness within the seeking lifestream.

Finally, that "Holy Christ Self", at the sincere, loving and constant invitation of the "outer self", takes complete command of that "personality" and "soul" and the individual then becomes an "Illumined One"—the Christ-in-action here in this physical appearance world (as Beloved Jesus was!).

Now, the reason for the Blue Plume always standing on the left, Gold in the center and Pink on the right, is this:

In the heart, the Blue Flame, representing energy, naturally would *receive* the life-essence as it flows into that Flame. Then It is passed through the Gold Plume of Wisdom and Illumination (in order to show the personality what the Presence desires done with Its life which It is giving so freely to the "outer self"). Then this energy is dispensed through the Pink Plume on the right side—representing the releasing of the blessings of Divine Love from the Father. This holds the perfect balance of that which is received, qualifying it for its right use (righteousness) and then dispensing it only as God would do so—through Divine Love!

It is perfectly obvious, of course, that when one would be standing *before* that Flame (or seeing someone standing within It) the colors of that Flame would seem to be reversed—but such would not be the case. Blue is *always* on the left and Pink *always* on the right— with the Gold Plume in the center.

The "Holy Christ Self"

The "Holy Christ Self" has been referred to as "The Higher Mental Body" of the individual lifestream and spoken of by our Beloved Jesus as "The Mediator between God and man". The "Holy Christ Self" represents the "only-begotten Son" of the Holy Trinity. In the Bible, (Psalm 121) it is referred to as "He that keepeth Israel (that which IS REAL about you—your God-individuality) shall neither slumber nor sleep".

The "Holy Christ Self" is the wholly perfect Christ-consciousness of each lifestream and has an anchorage within the Immortal Three-fold Flame of Eternal Truth of Divine Love, Wisdom and Power,—this focus of God's life being held within the physical heart of every individual and gives that heart the energy of beating.

While a focus of this Christ-Self is anchored within the physical heart of the "outer self", yet the greater part of this Christ-consciousness lives in Its Own Realms of Perfection and fulfills Its Own Divine Plan at Inner Levels. This Christ consciousness is the All-knowing Mind of God and, of course, possesses all the God-qualities of the All-Seeing-Eye and All-Hearing-Ear of God. Its God-intelligence can look both ways—up to the "I Am" Presence, seeing there that glorious God-perfection (for the "I Am" Presence is the One spoken of in the Bible (Habakkuk 1:13) as 'I AM of too pure eyes to behold iniquity'). The "Christ-Self" can also look down into the "personality" or "outer self" and see the shadowed world which it has created. However, the "Christ-Self" *knows* the *unreality* of those shadows and will not accept them into Its world.

When given opportunity so to do, through the call of the "outer self" to God for help, that "Holy Christ Self" reaches up into the Causal Body (the accumulation of Good which is stored in the bands of color around the "I Am" Presence (See explanation of "Causal Body") and draws forth for the personal self whatever good is needed to "make things right". Thus It brings balance, merciful release and relief into manifestation right here in the physical appearance world.

Until the "outer self" or "personality" really recognizes and accepts the Truth of its being—its Source—the "I AM" Presence, this "Holy Christ Self" has little, if any, opportunity *in a whole embodiment* to give much assistance to the "personality". However, once that Truth is acknowledged and the individual turns his consciousness back to his own "I AM" Presence again and again

(in daily rhythmic application of the Laws of
Life which he has learned) , then the "Holy Christ
Self" begins the expansion of Its light from within
the Three-fold Flame—expanding it through and
around the outer "personality". From then on,
little by little, It compels all into perfect Divine
Order through Divine Love in the being and world
of the "outer self".

In the spiritually unawakened, when a lifestream
comes into embodiment, the "Holy Christ Self"
releases the life energy which flows through it to
the "outer self" at a "set" rate of vibration and
speed, according to the karmic limitations which
that "outer self" has previously created for itself.
Until the consciousness of the individual has
reached the physical age of about eighteen years
(sometimes twenty-one and sometimes even twenty-
eight) , the "Holy Christ Self" is not too much
concerned with the activities of the "personality".
However, as the individual matures to the ages
mentioned above this "Christ Self" then endeavors
to take more control of the world of that individual
—as much as the free-will of the "personality" will
permit. Sometimes this is very little, if any, and
great distress ensues as a result of this lack of co-
operative partnership.

However, the very moment the individual becomes consciously aware of the Truth of his being
—that he came forth from his own individualized
"I AM" Presence and that the fulfillment of his
Divine Plan and goal of all his existence is to

return to that Presence in the Ascension—from
that moment on the "Holy Christ Self" "neither
slumbers nor sleeps". It constantly watches the
"personality" and It gives tremendous assistance to
that one in his struggle to be free from the binding
chains and creations of his mistaken use of God's
perfect life—flowing into him every moment, so
freely and so perfect. Finally, after *enough* use of
the Violet Transmuting Flame has been used and
the causes and cores of human mistakes have been
completely removed, and replaced by constructive
activities and creations, then the "Holy Christ
Self" takes complete and eternal possession of all
the consciousness and energy of the "personality"
and absorbs that consciousness into Itself. This is
the beginning of the Ascension into the "I AM"
Presence of all the energies of the entire lifestream.
Blessed be the "Holy Christ Selves" of all mankind
and may They quickly render this freeing service
to all the lifestreams through whose hearts They
have allowed life to beat.

Recently the Great Cosmic Law has permitted
the Great Lord Maitreya (former World Teacher
and now the New Buddha for this Earth) to issue
a Divine Fiat to the effect that the "Holy Christ
Self" *now* was permitted to remove from the "outer
self" all destructive use of its free-will and thus take
complete and eternal command more quickly.
This will greatly hasten the evolution of this
Planet and all belonging to It—releasing It into
God-freedom in the Light—the perfection which It

had and knew with the Father in the beginning—
"before the world was"!

The "Personality"

The "personality" (sometimes referred to as "the
outer self") is just exactly what this latter term
implies—the outer consciousness of the individual
lifestream which has forgotten its Divine Source
and thought itself apart from God *which condition,
of course, is utterly impossible*—since GOD IS
LIFE and the life of the "outer self" or "personality" is God's life!

Therefore, the "outer self" is that which has
cognized (for the most part) only the appearances
in his own world and the world with which he is
surrounded. This "outer self" is cognized and
associated with by others of the same consciousness
in contrast to the "Inner Self" or "Christ consciousness", a living focus of which is anchored within
the physical heart within the Immortal Three-fold
Flame which is there—the energy of which gives
the physical heart the ability to beat. This "Inner
Self" is not seen by the physical sight or heard by
the physical ear of the *spiritually unawakened*
individual. This "Inner Self" has sometimes been
referred to as "The still, small voice within".

The word "personality" stems from the Greek
word "personnae" which refers to a "mask". In
the early days of the theatre, only men and boys
were used as actors to portray the various char-

acters and masks were used to express various human emotions, i.e., sadness, laughter, surprise, etc. Many times, in listing the cast of characters in a play, above the list of names will appear the words "Dramatis Personnae"—meaning "the 'dramatic masks' which will appear in this play". Thus, the "personality" is the humanly created "mask" over the perfection of one's *Individuality*—that *Individuality* always having been and always remaining PERFECT!

The God-perfection of the Light Pattern of the individual can never be changed or despoiled in any way! Human discordant shadows can only be imposed upon that Light—shutting in Its glorious radiance, beauty and God-perfection. This has been done by mankind's forgetfulness of the Source of God-light, God-life and God-love from whence he came. Now, by the use of the transcendent gift of the Violet Fire of Divine Love, Transmutation, Mercy and Compassion, man again has opportunity to purify the shadows which he has created in the past and NOW transmute them into Light.

Then, by the *correct* use of the creative word "I AM" (which is the Name of God Himself— (Exodus 3:14)), he may build his world anew and attain eternal mastery in the victory of his ascension into Light. This is the Immortal Goal of every lifestream on this planet or any other—the Ascension in the Light! The Ascended Master Jesus Christ accomplished this victory and attained

His Own Ascension by the faithful use of the same Laws which He and the Other Great Ones are teaching us today and did He not say: "The things that I have done SHALL YE DO ALSO!"?

The "Soul"

The Law of Re-embodiment is a Cosmic Law and It continues to act, century after century, age after age—*whether mankind believes in Its existence or not!* Like the Law of "electricity", *it just is and always has been* and ignorance of its presence in the Universe or disbelief of its existence cannot possibly cause it to cease to be or act. *It is and it acts!* Even in the outer world, most of us are familiar with the phrase "Ignorance of the Law is no excuse".

In each embodiment (and every one living on Earth today has had thousands of them—some long and some shorter of duration) the individual creates for himself a "personality"—the consciousness which the individual develops as a result of all his experiences of that life-span. (See explanation of "personality").

The "soul" is the aggregate consciousness of all the "personalities" which one has created by the use of the God-life which has been allotted to him —ever since the "fall of man". *This "fall" was in consciousness* and came about through his complete *ignor*-ance and forgetfulness of his Source.

This forgetfulness of his Source and Divine Pattern and Plan for embodiment here resulted in the distortion of that Plan and Its resultant creation of imperfection.

"Save my soul" is often heard in the prayers of Orthodox channels. What that phrase really means is: "Purify all my life's energy which I have misqualified by imposing upon it the shadows of human ignorance and mistakes". The sooner the soul of the individual is so "saved" (redeemed) by the purifying action of the Sacred Fire directed into and through it, the better it is for the individual who, by his forgetfulness of his Divine Source, has become caught in a maze of human creations and knows not how to free himself.

When a sincere call for help of any kind goes up to God from a lifestream in distress, that help is instantly at hand—given by the Ascended Masters, Angelic Host and other loving and all-powerful Messengers of God Who live but to do His Will and endeavor to raise all life into Their Own Mastery and Perfection. "Call unto Me and I will answer you . . ."; "Ask and ye shall receive. . . ."; "Come unto Me. . . ." THE FIRST MOVE MUST COME FROM THE ONE IN NEED, since that need only arose because of his departure from Perfection—BY HIS OWN CHOICE—somewhere along life's pathway. Now, he must consciously "turn about face" and WANT TO KNOW how to "make things right".

The "Tube of Light" Protection

Since we have all been reminded often of the
Chinese wisdom which tells us that "One picture
is worth ten thousand words!", we can but suggest
to our Gentle Readers that, if they have not
already seen one, they procure as quickly as possible a copy of THE CHART OF THE INDI-
VIDUALIZED PRESENCE OF EACH LIFE-
STREAM, Whose Divine God-Name is "I AM"
(Bible—Exodus 3:14).

In the beginning of a lifestream's spiritual
awakening, this "Tube" of pure, electronic light
essence may be drawn down about the four lower
bodies by the personality, at his call to his own
"I AM" Presence in which he lives, moves and has
his actual being. The greater part of the consciousness of one's own God-self lives in Its Own
Higher Consciousness of Absolute Perfection,
while a focus of that Perfection is anchored by the
Holy Christ Self within the Three-fold Flame within each beating heart. (See explanation of "Three-
fold Flame" previously described herein). Quite
naturally, ALL of the God-Presence "I AM" (or
even of the Holy Christ Self) could not be and
is not anchored within the physical heart—*else
would the outer self or personality be wholly perfect!* Whatever Perfection *is there* has had the
shadows of discordant human thought, feeling,
spoken word and deed imposed upon It, shutting
in Its Divine radiance—all of this instruction

having been set forth in detail heretofore in this book.

However, as the consciousness of the individual awakens and his "inner light" has expanded sufficiently, the radiation of light from the Three-fold Flame within his heart expands until Its light meets that of the Tube of Light and the individual then becomes self-luminous—"transfigured" as Beloved Jesus was on the Mount of Transfiguration.

By holding the thoughts, feelings, spoken words and actions of the personality or "outer self" wholly harmonious (if only for forty-eight hours continuously at one time) one could make this Tube of Light protection an invincible wall of invisibility, invincibility and invulnerability about one and nothing of the discords of the outer world, other personalities or conditions could possibly disturb the one so protected. This may be proven to be very effective if one wishes to try it!

(See p. 21 of August 1956 "Bridge" for more explanation of the Tube of Light and statement for Its daily use.)

Now, if one should become discordant and lose his self-control (perhaps because of some old momentums of destructive habits of feeling), one should immediately call on the Law of Forgiveness saying: "Beloved Presence of God 'I AM' in me, 'I Am' the Ascended Masters' Law of Forgiveness, Forgetfulness and Transmuting Flame of this mistake which I have made, all the mistakes

I have ever made and those of all mankind; as well as those of the Elemental Kingdom. Transmute this misqualified energy into 'The Light of God that NEVER fails'. Illumine our minds and feelings and see that neither I nor any of the rest of life ever make that or any other mistake again". Then use the statement calling for the "Tube of Light" protection again to be established about you.

Be sure to call for this "Tube of Light" protection every morning before you leave your room or home for the day. While giving the statement, picture a Tube of dazzling white light substance (like sun on glistening snow) pouring down around you as a circular wall of light; this light essence constantly pouring like a Niagara Falls. See this "Tube" to be about nine feet in diameter and about three feet thick.

This "Tube of Light" may be given the color of any one of the Seven Rays; It may be charged with your favorite fragrance from the flower of your choice and It may also be charged to carry some favorite melody which you would like all to hear as you approach. For instance, as the Beloved Jesus appears, the melody of "Joy to the World" is heard in the atmosphere.

After a short time of faithfully calling forth this activity of the "Tube of Light" protection, one will be able to *feel the benefit* of Its use and will wonder how he ever got along without It.

Here is a suggested short form for the calling

forth of this "Tube"—as stated above, there is a much more efficacious form available for this purpose in the August, 1956 "Bridge":

"Beloved Mighty Victorious Presence of God 'I AM' in me! Blaze Thou around me now Thy invincible Cosmic Christ protection of the Tube of pure electronic Light essence. See to it for me that this protection is all-powerfully active and eternally sustained. Let no human discordant creation ever reach me through It. Let this Tube of Light essence make and keep me invisible and invulnerable to every human shadow, constantly raising and holding my attention upon Thy Omnipresence—in everyone, everything, everywhere. I consciously accept this done RIGHT NOW with full power."

The Violet Transmuting Flame

(Also known as "The Freedom Flame")

The tender solicitous love of the Father-Mother God of this Universe for Their children is perhaps most plainly shown by Their gift to those children of the use of the Violet Transmuting Flame. When consciously called into dynamic action in, through and around the individual, Its gracious presence and power are so far-reaching in Its merciful release from the penalties incurred by the discordant use of life's energies, that Its full meaning and blessing seem quite incredible to the average individual, especially when It is brought to his outer attention for the first time. However, those who are very sincere and wise will instantly and joyously seize this opportunity to "make things right" by the daily use of this Flame.

In a very short time, if It is persistently and consistently called into action at least three times a day, the one so using It will begin to feel a much "lighter" atmosphere about him and many distressing conditions of body, mind, affairs and association will adjust themselves and those annoyances will fall away as if they had never been. *Anyone can prove this for himself, if he will!*

Within every God-intelligence there is the power to master his own life! You see, life is energy— light essence—which flows constantly in rhythm from the heart of one's own individualized "I AM" Presence. It flows into his physical heart and gives to that heart its energy and rhythm of beating.

In its primal state, that life is pure and perfect until it is used by the individual into whom it flows to make some form (determined by his thought) and then energized and made a living thing by the pouring of his feelings into it. When these creations are constructive, they make light, beautiful, happy forms in and around one's aura and they not only radiate their own blessings to their creator, but act as magnets to draw like vibrations and forms from all they contact.

The opposite of this activity is also true and, here, man comes to a place where the daily conscious calling forth of the Violet Transmuting

Flame of Divine Compassion, Forgiveness and Mercy is so essential. Depressed and destructive thoughts, feelings, spoken words and actions create such forms in the individual's world also and that individual, feeling resentment, injustice, pain, anger, etc. concerning them, fills those forms with the destructive rates of vibration and makes them live.

If the individual does not know how to protect himself against such forms in the worlds of others (by the use of the Tube of Light above referred to) then, since "like attracts like", one is drawn to persons, places, conditions and things of similar vibration, thus increasing the distress originally caused by the destructive use of his own free-will.

However, the tender, solicitous love of the Father-Mother God always provides a way out of all the difficulties into which Their children sometimes stray by a forgetfulness of the TRUE WAY, a desire to experiment with life or just a general rebellion in the feelings against giving obedience to the constructive way of life and a determination to have their own way. The Violet Transmuting Flame is that way out, proving Itself absolutely reliable and helpful beyond all words to describe, to all who care to try Its use.

How Do You Use This Violet Flame?

At least twice each day (and three times is even better!) go by yourself for at least fifteen minutes and make sure you are undisturbed during this time. Thoughtfully and sincerely use the statement provided later, endeavoring to picture the activity taking place just as and when you call It forth. Repeat the statement three times. Then keep your attention upon the activities of this Violet Fire, picturing It blazing all around you— rushing up from beneath your feet right up, in, through and around every cell and atom of the physical body, forming a pillar of Violet Fire about nine feet in diameter.

Without tension in the feelings, try to feel the power of this Violet Fire like a "blowtorch", instantly transmuting into light every discordant thought and feeling form which you have ever created, drawn about you or ever allowed to come into your world. Try it! It costs nothing to experiment with this wonderful God-friend of the ages. It cares nothing about your mistakes—Its only desire is to help you transmute them into light; bringing you comfort, peace and a sense of general well-being as It does so.

Give this Violet Flame an opportunity to show you what Its great loving heart of Mercy and Love wants to do for you. Use the above exercise faithfully for at least thirty days. Never miss one "treatment" and prove to yourself what a mighty assistance has been given you by your own God-presence—the Source of your very life. (For further instruction on the use of the Violet Transmuting Flame, please see "The Bridge to Freedom", July 1955, 1956 and 1957, pages 16, 21 and 21 respectively).

Here is suggested a short decree for one's use of this Violet Fire, but a more all-inclusive decree (which is far more effective) may be found for use in the July, 1956 issue of "The Bridge to Freedom".

"Beloved Presence of God 'I AM' in me, Beloved Saint Germain—Cosmic Freedom to our Earth—and All Who serve on the Seventh Ray:

SEAL, SEAL, SEAL me and every individual belonging to Earth's evolutions still unascended (whoever and wherever they may be), in a gigantic blazing pillar of the Freedom Flame of Violet Fire, in all transmuting Cosmic power, doubled each instant of each hour. Let this focus be eternally sustained, all-powerfully active and ever-expanding around each one, day and night, waking or sleeping; transmuting the cause and core of all destructive etheric records and all human mistakes, cause, effect, record and memory, into peace, health, happiness and the limitless supply of every good thing which God intended all He created to enjoy from the beginning. I consciously accept this done—RIGHT NOW— with full power!

Concerning Our Songs

In order to give our Gentle Readers a complete record of all that transpired in the classes which allowed the preceding addresses of the Seven Mighty Elohim to come forth into this physical octave, we are presenting the lyrics of the songs used in those meetings. These lyrics came forth from the Ascended Master Hilarion, Beloved Chohan of the Fifth Ray. They are meant to be either read or sung—they are *really* decrees set to harmonious rhythm and, if and when the melodies or musical accompaniments are not available to the Reader or student, these lyrics may be used as just spoken adorations to the Great Beings for Whom they are meant.

You will note that many of the melodies are marked "Original" but many are written to the tunes of familiar songs which people have enjoyed through the years. These words will lift the vibratory action of those songs and all who have written or used them. We have used these melodies so that the songs could be sung more quickly than having to wait for the publishing of the original melodies—which, incidentally, is a slow and expensive process.

Some of the original melodies are now available on musical recordings (see advertising pages in back of book) and the others will be recorded as quickly as we are able to do so.

BELOVED SANAT KUMARA

Sanat Kumara, Gracious Lord and King—
   Before Your Throne, our homage now we bring:
Offerings and gifts of humble service true,
   Reverence and gratitude to God for You!

Humbly we bow before Your glorious Throne,
   Clothe us in love and make us all Your Own!
Give us Your courage, strength and patience rare;
   Flood through us Venus' love for all to share.

Flood us with light, sustain us by Your power;
   Give us Your wisdom, guide us every hour;
Seal us in peace—in love's Own God-control;
   Let Your great Wings of Love our worlds enfold.

You are God's glory, majesty and grace!
   Your patient care has held for Earth Her place.
All through the ages that have gone before—
   Your love has been for Earth the Open Door.

Now lift our Earth from strain and stress today;
   Free all Her life—so earnestly we pray!
Forces of Nature, Elementals, too,
   Sanat Kumara, dear! ALL call to You!

Glory and honor unto You belong!
   Let all men free You now in grateful song!
Let all that lives upon this Planet raise
   Heart, soul and spirit to Your Name in praise!

Great Central Sun, Your gifts of love we call
   For our dear Friend of Light and Lord of All!
Bless His dear Venus—Goddess from the Sun;
   Bless Their dear Planet and all life thereon!

(HYMN TUNE: "Abide With Me")

(Song referred to on p. 161)

OUR MARY DEAR

Our Mary Dear, we love Thee so—
    Now draw us "Home" by love!
Make each an arm of Thy great Self,
    Through us love's healing prove.
Make us Thy great Forgiveness,
    Thy beauty and Thy peace;
Expand Thy light from Heaven's height
    'Til all life finds release.

O Mary, our Beloved One—
    Our hearts are Thine today!
Accept us now as low we bow,
    Walk through us all Earth's way.
Make us Love's healing presence
    Of God's great Plan fulfilled;
Show all Thy face; flood forth Thy grace,
    Until all storms are stilled.

O Mary, Jesus, Joseph, too,
    Release love's new rebirth;
Bring forth the Holy Family
    In every home on earth!
Establish there the glory
    Of God's great Three-fold Flame!
Make all desire the Sacred Fire—
    USED ONLY IN GOD'S NAME!

(HYMN TUNE: "O Little Town of Bethlehem")

(Song referred to on p. 101)

MAGNIFY THE LORD

Blessed Mother Mary, from Your glorious height,
  Come into our hearts and fill our worlds with Light;
Make us truly grateful for our Victory won—
  Help us magnify the Lord, as You have done!

Chorus:
Magnify the Lord, O soul of me!
  Magnify the Lord for all to see!
Magnify Him; Glorify His name!
  Gratitude will raise ALL on Ascension's Flame!

All the Hosts of Heaven (such a glorious throng)
  Angel choirs and voices join our happy song;
All throughout the Universe the word has spread—
  "Earth has turned from shadows—Loves her God instead!"

All mankind shall one day know the Truth of Life;
  Violet Fire shall have transmuted storm and strife;
All evolving on the Earth shall use "The Word"—
  Purify with Light and magnify the Lord!

FINAL CHORUS:

Purify my soul, O Flame "I Am"!
  Purify my soul by Christ command!
Purify me! Glorify Thy Name!
  Purify and raise *all* on Ascension's Flame!

Chorus to use when calling for others:
Purify their souls, O Flame of them!
  Purify their souls and raise all men!
Purify them! Glorify Thy Name—
  Purify and raise all on Ascension's Flame!

(HYMN TUNE: "Count Your Blessings")

(Song referred to on p. 131)

228

BEAUTIFUL KWAN YIN

There comes to my heart one sweet Name,
  The blessing of Mercy's Love Flame;
I sing it again and again—
  Kwan Yin! the gift of God's Love.

CHORUS:

Kwan Yin! Kwan Yin!
  Goddess of Mercy above;
O beautiful, lovely Kwan Yin!
  God's Flame of Merciful Love.

Her Mercy of love is divine;
  To Her, doubts and fears I resign;
I claim Her forgiveness as mine—
  So help me, blessed Kwan Yin.

Her mercy of love is so sweet;
  It makes the soul's victory complete;
It brings all the world to Her feet;
  Kwan Yin—the Mercy of Love.

(HYMN TUNE: "Sweet Peace, the Gift of God's Love")
(Song referred to on p. 99).

BELOVED ARCHANGEL MICHAEL

Archangel Michael, how glorious You are!
  Help us redeem our dear Earth, "The Dark
    Star";
Bring us Your Legions of Angels to heal,
  Prosper, illumine,—God's love to reveal.

CHORUS:

We love You, our Archangel Michael!
  Come, Cherubim—Join in our song!
A Sponsor of Love's Golden Cycle—
  Come! Sing His praise all the day long;
And Seraphim in shining glory,
  Bring all of God's Light from above!
His Presence we claim; on wings of Blue Flame
  Comes Archangel Michael, OUR LOVE!

Archangel Michael, our Darling of Light,
  Sever Earth's bonds by Your Sword of great
    might!
Lift all mankind from mistakes of the past;
  Raise all the Earth from the shadows at last.

Archangel Michael we're grateful to You—
  Ne'er could we ever repay all You do!
Thank You for loving us, setting us free—
  Fulfill God's Plan through us all, constantly!

(MELODY: Original)

(Song referred to on p. 133)

LOVE'S OPPORTUNITY

There is a Goddess so precious,
  Earth's atmosphere She commands;
Gifts of opportune action,
  Holding in Her hopeful hands.

CHORUS:

Love's opportunity
  Brings all God's gifts to all men;
Love's opportunity's calling—
  Calling again and again.

She comes in many disguises,
  Not always blazing Her light;
Only vibration apprises
  What's to be done that is right.

Beware the sins of omission,
  Often more grievous than wrong;
Though the sin be forgiven,
  Yet the blessing is gone!

Justice is love's opportunity,
  Holding wide God's Open Door.
Take from the hands of this Goddess
  Blessings of good held in store.

(HYMN TUNE: "There Shall Be Showers of Blessings")

(Song referred to on p. 100)

The Ascended Master Teaching Foundation

The Ascended Master Teaching Foundation (AMTF) was founded in response to the call of the Ascended Masters Saint Germain and El Morya for co-workers to assist Their efforts on behalf of mankind and this planet. It was decided that the plan of the Masters - as given in the 1930's and 1950's through the messengers Guy Ballard and Geraldine Innocenti - could best be implemented by adopting the following plan of action:

1) Gathering all of the original dictations given through these two messengers

2) Categorizing and summarizing these dictations, numbering about 15,000 pages, but leaving the original message intact, and not adding personal opinions or concepts

3) Publicizing the original material, when possible, making it freely available, without restrictions

4) Translating this information into other languages in accordance with the wishes of the Masters

5) Giving interested persons the opportunity of forming study groups. These groups have two main objectives. They enrich the students' knowledge of Ascended Master teaching, and they offer the students a vehicle in giving a balance to Life by sending energy to the Masters. This is done through decrees, songs and visualizations. The latter activity assists the Divine Beings in increasing their much needed service on behalf of this planet. These study groups are to operate independently and free from outside direction. Each group is to be guided by the wishes and individual talents of its members, the common bond being the instructions of the Ascended Masters as given to the two messengers.

Individuals ready to put the shoulder to the wheel and join El Morya's Spiritual Caravan - an effort fully supported by Saint Germain and the other members of the Great White Brotherhood - are invited to become co-workers. Write for the free leaflet "Ascended Master Teaching, the Teaching of the New Age", AMTF P.O. Box 466, Mount Shasta, CA. 96067.

BOOKS DISTRIBUTED BY AMTF

MAN, HIS ORIGIN, HISTORY AND DESTINY by W. Schroeder, 336 pp. Using a variety of sources, this new title presents mankind's unrecorded history. Much of the material has not been researched before, and it has not been available to the general public. Written in chronological order, the reader learns of the conditions prevailing during the advent of man on Earth, including his origin and his age. Fascinating highlights of the Lemurian and Atlantean civilizations are given. Also depicted are accounts of the unchronicled history of Jesus and the oracles of Delphi. Practical solutions are presented to meet   today's planetary crisis. $10.00

UNVEILED MYSTERIES by Godfre Ray King, 288 pp. This book contains Mr. Ballard's group of first experiences, following his meeting with the Ascended Master Saint Germain on Mount Shasta. We are happy to present to the students a full, unabridged copy of this priceless book, which heralded in the New Age.$9.75

THE FIRST RAY by the Ascended Master El Morya, 128 pp. Herein are described the God-Virtues of the First Ray, how the dispensation for the "Bridge to Freedom" was obtained, and the purpose of this endeavor. In the section "The Spiritual Caravan" El Morya extends an invitation to students to join him in a global effort, bringing in a New Golden Age. $5.75

THE SEVEN MIGHTLY ELOHIM SPEAK ON THE SEVEN STEPS TO PRECIPITATION by Thomas Printz, 256 pp. This book contains the original account of the principles employed in the creation of our planet by the Builders of the Universe, known as the Seven Elohim. The principles of precipitation are part of the eternal Law of Life. Therefore man, as Co-Creator with God, may utilize them to his advantage in his daily affairs. $9.45

THE SEVENTH RAY by the Ascended Master Saint Germain, 128 pp. This book consists of several addresses by Saint Germain. Featured are primal requirements for an efficacious service, and the responsibilities of each group member, including its leader. An indispensable aid for those involved in group activities. $5.75

MEMOIRS OF BELOVED MARY, MOTHER OF JESUS by Thomas Printz, 192 pp. Chronicled here are several addresses by Mary, depicting details of her last embodiment, with Jesus. Many of these are not given in the Bible, such as early life experiences of Jesus, his trip to India, and details of his ascension. The reader learns of Mary's journey to Europe, including her travels to Fatima, Lourdes and Glastonbury. $8.00

THE SEVEN BELOVED ARCHANGELS SPEAK, 136 pp. Each of the seven Archangels radiates one of the virtues of the Godhead, such as protection, illumination and peace. This book contains a personal address from each of these Great Beings, showing the reader how to use these virtues for achieving their own freedom. $5.90

I AM DISCOURSES by Mighty Victory. This tall Master from Venus embodies the God-Virtue of Victorious Accomplishment. He has offered to assist students to manifest this God-Quality in their daily affairs, 320 pp. $10.90

CONTROL OF THE ELEMENTS by Thomas Printz, 24 pp. The reader is acquainted with the nature of elemental life and he learns how to protect himself from earthquakes, volcanic activities and violent storms. $2.00

THE GREAT WHITE BROTHERHOOD, 90 minute tape. Talk by W. Schroeder at "Light Ages Symposium", Harvard University, May 1987 $6.00

BRIDGE TO FREEDOM JOURNAL. The original dictations of the Ascended Masters as published in the monthly magazine of the "Bridge to Freedom" activity, bound, approx. 260 pp. each. Most of these messages, as listed in the Journals and Bulletins, cannot be found in any other book. They are a practical guide, leading to spiritual development and a better understanding of the activities of the Ascended Ones.

Vol. I & II 4/1952 to 3/1954   Total $15.90
Vol. III & IV 4/1954 to 3/1956   Total $16.90
Vol. V to VI 4/1956 to 3/1958   Total $16.90

BRIDGE TO FREEDOM BULLETINS. The original dictations of the Masters of Wisdom as published on a weekly basis, approx. 300 pp. each.

Vol. I & II 4/1952 to 3/1954   Total $16.90
Vol. III & IV & V 4/1954 to 3/1957   Total $16.90
Vol. VI & VII 4/1957 to 3/1959   Total $16.90

PICTURES AND KEYNOTES OF ASCENDED MASTERS. These are effective tools of attunement. Write for information.

MIRACLES OF TODAY. Personal experiences in applying Ascended Master Teaching, by Saint Germaine's appointed messenger, W. Cassiere, 80 pp. $3.00

HEALING HANDS. A healing technique to apply to many situations, by W. Cassiere, 20 pp. $1.00

ORDERING INFORMATION:

Write to AMTF, P.O. Box 466, Mount Shasta, CA 96067. Delivery charges. U.S.: $2.50 first copy, $0.50 each additional book; other countries: $3.00 first copy, $1.00 each additional book. Sales tax 6%, California residents only.

FOR NEW PRICES
SEND FOR BOOKLIST